Dodge It If You Can

Aw Yang Uei

David Mouland

ISBN: 979-867-31684-3-1

CONTENTS

ACKNOWLEDGEMENTS

'I would like to thank Aw for coming up with the idea and having the motivation to get it started. I would like to thank the girl in the restaurant in the beer dress for distracting us from the current project that we were working on and should have been talking about over dinner, and for the beer. I would like to thank my mum whose immediate reaction when I told her I was collaborating on a book about my work was 'Who's going to read that?' Finally, I would like to thank all the fantastic people we talk about in the stories who, however much we may appear to disparage them through our story telling, are all unique and wonderful characters and people without whose opinions, actions, successes and mistakes the human race could never progress. You can only learn from mistakes, if you never make a mistake then your job is too easy.' – David Mouland

'I would like to thank David for agreeing to the idea and keeping the pressure on me to finish writing all the chapters. As a snail-paced writer, the invisible peer pressure did help to get me moving. I wasn't sure about the distraction he got in the restaurant: I was too focused on discussing ideas with him. I completely missed that distraction, must have been a phenomenon. I want to thank all the people who have crossed paths with me: I have learnt so much from all of them. I wrote all the stories from my heart and I hope you will learn from our mistakes. I would like to thank Cecelia Alphonsus for giving us many ideas: having a quote from Star Trek at the beginning of each chapter was one of the awesome ideas from her. I would like to thank Kenneth Shee, who gave us such helpful advice and encouragement. I want to thank you for investing your time in reading this book, I hope it will serve you well.' – Aw Yang Uei

i

A SPECIAL THANK YOU

Heartfelt thanks to Koen Olie who contributed all the beautifully articulated drawings in this book.

Koen graduated from Comenius College in the Netherlands and, due to his voracious reading habits, started working in a bookshop and from there continued into the publishing industry. He started travelling in the early 1980s through Europe and Asia, but kept coming back to Thailand and finally settled there in 1987, supporting his Thai family through teaching English and drawing.

During the '90's his (non-digital) illustrations and cartoons appeared in local Thai magazines and newspapers as well as in a few books for local publishers.

In the same period he met David when they started working for the same language institute. Over the years they always kept in touch and exchanged stories, some of which can be found in this book!

In 2003 he moved from education to tourism and has been actively working for a local DMC (Destination Management Company) ever since.

Olie still starts sketching on paper, but scans and works on it afterwards with photoshop, resulting in a kind of hybrid old school/digital art, a technique which was used for this great collection of almost true short stories.

For more art and photography search for 'art58koen' or visit https://artkoen.wixsite.com/artkoen

THE STORY BEHIND THE STORIES

Aw and I were in Kuala Lumpur one evening, I think in January 2020, having dinner at a classic Chinese restaurant, one of those places designed for large parties such as weddings, retirements, staff parties or bar mitzvahs. Thinking about it, they probably don't have bar mitzvahs in Malaysia.

It was an enormous room with hundreds of tables and a stage at one end. Since it was so often used for wedding receptions the decorations were always left in place regardless of whether a wedding was on or not, giving the place an aura of permanent romance. We sometimes went to this restaurant when I was in town on a business trip and it was either crammed full because of a party or otherwise completely empty.

We got a table and ran through the wine list with the aim of selecting a not too expensive bottle of red. However, a pretty girl wearing a tight dress obviously loaned to her by a well-known beer company took our attention and we ended up having beer. Over the beer and the food, we chatted about our normal topics which ranged from work to Star Trek to Game of Thrones and, often as not, back to Star Trek again. Our conversations often led to nostalgic stories of prior experiences (Captain's Log stories) which were related, sometimes very tentatively, to the issues we were facing at the current time. Generally, the more beer, the more tentative the story's relationship to the current situation and the more tragic, 'please beam me out of here' tales they became.

During one such exchange, Aw told me that he had had the idea just recently of writing a book on our swapped anecdotes. Logically, writing a book about the supply chain witterings of two tipsy old men should lead only to the ultimate cure for insomnia. However, I'd had a few beers and so thought it was a great idea.

I never expected to receive Chapter One a couple of weeks later from Aw. Feeling conscientious about not having done anything, I took inspiration from Aw's story and wrote my own first chapter and sent it back. Thus, began a story swap of increasing frequency, helped along by the onset of the Coronavirus pandemic that left both of us with more time than usual on our hands.

Within just a couple of months we had completed it and Aw had even found a publisher (Aw's coronavirus lockdown in Malaysia was significantly more intense than the one I experienced in Hong Kong so I can only assume he was suffering from severe boredom).

So here it is, the supply chain babblings of beer drinkers, something to help you sleep at night. Hope you enjoy!

David Mouland
30 May 2020

When David and I met in the office, we would often get distracted by many other matters. Therefore, having dinner together provided a much-needed quality discussion time when we could speak freely on the projects both of us were involved with.

After our discussions, usually facilitated by wines or beers or sometimes a bit of both, we liked to roam freely on topics from outer space to time travel to President Trump to Game of Thrones, and eventually we always landed on Star Trek.

That night when we decided to write this book together, with the effect of beers, we jokingly named this book on the spot. I called it 'Some bullets we've dodged!' and David immediately added 'and some we didn't!'

We agreed to write stories that were at least half a decade old when our paths had not yet crossed. We agreed to avoid writing anything about recent years, and we both strongly agreed that it would be an excellent idea to leave something for the two old men to do when they get older.

The temporary book title 'Some bullets we've dodged and some we didn't!' was in giant font size on the first page of our manuscript until we had finished writing the entire book. All the chapters were in the original order of sequence when we exchanged our writing. I wrote chapter 1 and sent it to David, he responded with chapter 2, and then I answered him with chapter 3, and thus began our writing journey.

At one time, we thought of using the classic bullet dodging scene from the movie, Matrix, as the book cover, replacing Keanu Reeves with our photos.

I told David it would look very cool for he is far more charming and good looking than Keanu; he squinted with a smile, I believe he agreed with me in that instance.

We finished writing all the chapters about the end of May, 2020.

When I read the book again, I enjoyed it and I hope you will enjoy the book as much as we do.

The book title has turned out to be one of our biggest challenges. At the time of writing this, we are still toying with the title, which is fun but I am really looking forward to making up our minds.

Aw Yang Uei
18 June 2020

1

THE UNATTRACTIVE VASE

'Things are only impossible until they're not.'
-- Captain Jean-Luc Picard

'You just need to be there, and you don't even need to speak a lot. There may be some IT questions for you but nothing that you can't handle. Just be there for three days,' said my ex-boss.

That was a simple, straightforward and unexciting 20-second sales pitch. The offer was for me to appear in a meeting as a not very attractive vase for three days.

'Who will be at the meeting?'
'Two senior consultants from the software company and a few warehouse managers. Don't worry! It will be easy. The consultants will take care of everything.'

'Why don't you attend yourself?'
'I want to, but I've another appointment in Singapore. Look, don't worry, you can handle this.'

That was it. I was being put in a three-day detailed warehouse-management functional meeting with one of the top multi-national third-party logistics companies. The company was building a 300,000 square-foot distribution centre in Shah Alam, Malaysia and the new facility was to be shared by three of their big customers, hence they required a high-end WMS (Warehouse Management System). At that time, that warehouse would be one of the first state-of-the-art multifunction distribution centres in Malaysia.

The problem? I was being sold into the project as an IT warehouse-software expert, but back then, I had zero experience in warehouses and logistics. My experience at that time was in electronic procurement and cybersecurity.

My ex-boss is one of the best businessmen I have ever known. He was a friend of the regional sales director of the WMS, and he saw the business opportunity and wanted to be the reseller of this Australian-made WMS. He had no suitable resources to attend the meeting, so he called me, two days before the big day.

So, I made a quick decision – a weird one. I agreed to the arrangement on the spot, no further phone calls or clarifications were required. He told me the time and venue, and I committed to being there for the meeting.

I thought about how my decision was made for years afterwards. I concluded that it was on my overwhelming curiosity about how raw materials were acquired and moved to factories, and how finished products were moved in the supply chain; the decision was made simply by my 'gut feel'.

Once the decision was made, I had only a day to learn about warehouse and logistics. At that time, the Internet was still in its infancy and there was no YouTube, no smartphone, and Google was not popular. Yahoo was my default search engine, but there were not many reading materials available online. I visited some bookstores and tried to read as much as I could.

Just a day to prepare myself was certainly not enough. I could barely scratch the supply-chain surface by reading all the available books I could find. I can still remember the feeling of butterflies in my stomach on the day of the meeting. I felt like I was walking into a kill zone and I was hoping and praying hard that I could dodge all the bullets.

The attendees were the Vice President of Operations, a Senior Solution Architect, six Senior Warehouse Managers, three Senior

Contract Managers and two WMS experts from Australia.

These were all heavyweights in their respective areas, and I had just entered the most critical meeting in the history of their organisation, setting up the best-in-class distribution centre in Malaysia.

The meeting was very intense and the project had a very tight timeline. The WMS needed to be installed; people needed to be trained to use the system; the software needed to be configured and tuned to what was agreed in the meeting, so as to govern the processes of the warehouse operations; different reports required various customisations; the key performance indicator reports needed to be built; the cycle count procedures needed to be confirmed; and all questions on RF operations needed answers.

But for me, the million-dollar question was '*What the heck is RF?*' As an IT expert, all the RF questions were directed to me.

'What RF devices should we use?'
'How many RF points do we need?'

'Where should we mount the RF points?'

'Thank God the air conditioner is working very well today! If not, my whole body could have been drenched in cold sweat!' That was my first silent gratitude prayer of that day.

I needed to keep calm, but I could not be saying *just* anything. What to say? As I didn't even know what RF was, it was going to be very embarrassing.

My mind tried to flip through all the books I had read, desperately seeking clues that could help me get out of this situation. Or allow me to sound a bit intelligent. At least let me know what RF means! Inside me, I was crying for help.

I tried to search for words to say, something smart, something that could provide some discussion so that I could buy a bit more time. I needed to find a way to dodge the bullets. Before those words could be found, one of the Senior Warehouse Managers started to pull out the warehouse floor plan, laid it on the table and unfolded it.

Everyone started walking towards the floor plan.

'God has mercy. Thank you!' It was another loud silent gratitude prayer.

The group of experts was so excited when the floor plan was shown. They started discussing the details, they pointed at various areas on the floor plan, giving ideas and started talking amongst themselves.

They had forgotten about me entirely.

A few minutes later, I realised I had ultimately benefited from having all the highly intelligent people in the room, and they had provided all the answers to all the questions they had asked.

'Let's not use the old RF technology, we should start using WIFI now,' said Adam. He was a Dutchman, and one of the smartest people I had met.

So THAT was the meaning of RF, a wireless network, RF meant radio frequency!

My heart pounded so hard and so rapidly. I felt that I was dancing with my heartbeats. I was so excited and relieved. The network was one of my strengths and I could talk all day about this.

'God has more mercy!' I shouted out another silent gratitude prayer.

After about 15 minutes, these experts began to settle down, and I became the focal point again.

'What RF devices should we use?' said one of the senior managers.
'Are you allowed to choose? Usually, a company like yours should have a guideline from your HQ,' I answered calmly. 'Could you check preferred devices in your guideline so I can advise you on the availability?'

I reckoned I must have sounded like an expert.
'How many RF points do we need?'

I walked closer to the floor plan, looked at it for a few seconds, and answered, 'It is hard to tell right now. First, we need to know the HQ preferred devices as each brand is slightly different from one another.'

I observed the people in the room. When some of the experts started to nod, I knew I had said the right thing. So, I continued, 'Generally speaking, you will need about 12 to 18 access points, depending on the preferred brands, and whether or not you are allowed to use WIFI 802.11b technology. I agree with Adam that WIFI technology will provide more benefits, one of them being that it gives better signal coverage, so you will need fewer access points.'

From their earlier discussions, I figured that Adam wanted to use new technologies, but the top management wanted to make sure that everything would comply with the HQ guideline.

More people nodded, so I went on to say, 'Let's check with HQ on the preferred brands and vendors of the devices, then we can organise a site survey to determine the number of access points and the best places to mount them.'

Bingo! All of them agreed. Phew!

'Thank God these people are so smart!' I had lost count of the number of times I had said the prayers. I was truly blessed to be surrounded by a group of smart people.

By the end of each day of the three-day meeting, I felt very excited but, equally, exhausted. I had learnt so much and I wished it were a one-week meeting so I could learn more. I slept like a log every night, and I appeared fresh each morning, ready to learn more.

I had made friends with the best warehouse management and logistics service professionals in this region, and two WMS experts. They had been so comfortable with me that they wanted my full-time involvement in this project. Not only had I offered the service contract to set up their network infrastructure, I was involved in the WMS configuration and also sold them nearly 100 units of RF devices.

It was a challenging but highly successful project, and we were among the pioneers who deployed WIFI devices to a large warehouse and used 2D barcodes. I still keep in touch with some of them today; many of them continue to refer more business opportunities to me, and they are my best referrals.

This was the turning point of my career, and thus began my journey into the supply chain and logistics software business.

* * *

Opportunities may not always be measured in the form of money. Trust your gut feeling for it will lead you to something amazing; say YES to amazing opportunities.

'It is the moment of decision, that your destiny is shaped.' -- *Tony Robbins*

2

TRANSLATING ENGLISH INTO ENGLISH

'It is the lot of "man" to strive no matter how content he is.'

-- Spock

I started my career in the space industry as a production engineer making satellites and the nose cone for the Arianespace rocket. After being laid off, the norm for the industry in the United Kingdom at the time, I took a year off, travelling in Asia. I ended up in Thailand and decided not to go back.

I did part-time jobs teaching English for a language school and eventually ended up as a Resident English Language Instructor and Consultant (RELIC) at a large distribution company in Bangkok.

Teaching English to Thai people was very much translating the broken English spoken by one person into English that was understandable to everyone else, i.e. I was an English to English translator!

I was teaching salespeople and my strategy to get them to talk was to enquire about the challenges they faced each day in their jobs – people just love the opportunity to vent their frustrations. The main frustration of salespeople was that logistics people kept delivering late or delivering wrong and they could not understand how the warehouse could be so incompetent. It was a great source of frustration for salespeople because they were always receiving complaints from customers.

As a consequence of this I began providing English training at the warehouse where I asked the warehouse people what their greatest challenges were. Interestingly, the warehouse people complained mostly about the salespeople never keeping to the agreed delivery lead time and always seemed to require urgent orders, especially at month end when 50% of the sales orders came in on the very last week.

Each day I would translate the warehouse responses to the salespeople and the following day I would translate the salespeople's response to the warehouse people. It was quite fascinating that both departments of this company had no idea of the problems each other faced. Intriguingly when the two sides got together and spoke to each other in their native Thai language they were unable to communicate effectively; they failed to listen to each other.

When I spoke to them in English on the same subjects, they focused their attention more keenly. The consequence of all this was that service lead times were agreed and communicated to customers, sales orders at month end reduced slightly, relieving pressure on the warehouse and orders held up due to credit checks or inventory shortages were not blamed on the warehouse anymore.

My training role at the company expanded into recruitment and I was asked to find candidates for a third party logistics team. Prior to this the company had only provided a full service whereby the company would buy products, mostly from abroad, then sell and distribute them to customers. This was before the domination by the big retailers (or Modern Trade as they are called) and most customers were local wholesalers as well as mom-and-pop (small and family-owned business) convenience stores.

Diversifying into third party logistics was new and it meant only providing warehousing and delivery services, the sales services were managed by the product owner. The service proved popular and we quickly expanded the team and the business began to grow at an unprecedented speed.

The company hired a professional logistics manager, Paul, from Australia to help us. He brought with him an enormous amount of experience and immediately realised our processes and our systems were very substandard.

I was tasked to hire an ISO manager and an ISO supervisor so that we could implement ISO9001 within nine months. ISO essentially provides the framework for an operation to follow standard procedures and reporting including proper analysis of mistakes and complaints.

After two months I had hired the supervisor but just could not find a suitable ISO manager so Paul told me that having failed to find one, I would have to implement ISO 9001 at the warehouse myself. Having no knowledge of what ISO entailed or of the logistics processes involved was clearly not an excuse for Paul so my protestations fell on deaf ears.

Left with no alternative I studied it. I managed to get an ISO consultant to help us one day a week and he taught me the ISO requirements. Within nine months we had the audit and to the astonishment of everyone in the organisation we actually passed.

The business continued to grow but Paul's family wanted to return to Australia so a year later I received a phone call from Paul asking if I could head up the warehouse administration department.

I duly replied that I could do that.

Another ten minutes passed, and I got another call. 'David, can you take on the transport management of the transport department?'

I didn't know much about transport.

'I don't really know much about transport Paul,' I responded.

'I didn't ask you that, I asked you if you could manage the transport department,' Paul said.

Putting it like that I said yes, I could probably do that. Similar calls came throughout the day and by the end of it, the Resident English Language Instructor and Consultant was the Logistics Manager for one the largest consumer distribution companies in South East Asia.

A couple of weeks after starting I had a large festering cold sore at the corner of my mouth. It was quite hideous and very sore. Paul saw me and laughed. 'That's the stress!' he chortled. Thus, my hitherto easy-going stress-free existence was gone and I was now forever caught in the no-man's-land of distributor between the big guns of the customers demanding higher service levels and the even bigger guns of the principals, the brand owners, demanding cheaper rates. Logistics is the Catch-22 of all jobs where pleasing one side will displease the other and it's all so easy to end up displeasing both.

* * *

If the acronym for your job title is RELIC, don't stick around doing the same monotonous tasks until you are one. Don't be restricted by your job title or job description, expand your knowledge and take on responsibility even if you don't immediately get remunerated for it, at least it will make your job more challenging and interesting.

'We keep moving forward, opening new doors, and doing new things, because we're curious and curiosity keeps leading us down new paths.' -- Walt Disney

3

THAT OLD WAREHOUSE

'Improve a mechanical device and you may double productivity. But improve man, you gain a thousand-fold.'

-- *Khan Noonien Singh*

Ravi stood next to his office table and tapped his foot against the floor in agitation as the call he was currently placing rang for the umpteenth time. I glanced out of his office window into the open grounds of the warehouse's loading dock and saw only a few heads at work.

Our appointment was interrupted by his more pressing concerns.

'Hi Sir, I tried calling you a few times, but you didn't pick up the call. Where is the extra manpower you promised to deliver today?' Ravi said to the person who just answered his call.

Even without putting the call on speaker, I could hear a hoarse voice from the phone, 'Don't yell at me!'

'I am not yelling. You are the HR, and you promised to give me extra headcount today.'

'I don't have time for this,' the voice responded, irritation conveyed in his tone.

Either the room was too quiet, or the person over the phone had a natural loud voice, Ravi did not notice I was listening to their conversation.

'Hold on and listen for a minute, Sir,' Ravi pleaded.

There was an inaudible mumble at the other end of the call. After a few seconds of eerie silence, 'Go on, I don't have all day,' the voice stated.

Ravi began, 'The warehouse is very important and paramount to the success of this company's sales operations. We are currently under-staffed, and we need more hands. In recent times, the workload has been very heavy, and the labour resources are stretched out. We implore you to hire some workers to come to help out with the operation at the warehouse.'

'I'll see what I can do about that,' the voice replied.

'All right, I'd appreciate it if you could work on that soon.'
'You can't order me about on what to do,' the voice retorted.

After a few seconds of silence, I began to wonder if the call had ended, but just then, the voice continued, 'On second thought, if you are in such haste, I will send some scapegoats down to your warehouse to aid you in your menial tasks.'

I was not sure if I'd heard correctly, the word 'scapegoat'.

Ravi chuckled, 'You undermine the importance of the warehouse, Sir. Every task we perform here is methodical.'

'You have big words for someone at such a lowly position. I'll personally handpick a few errant people from the headquarters here and send them your way.'

'Oh, I'll prefer if you can hire someone who is experienced in the operations of a warehouse,' Ravi pleaded.

'Come on! I'm sure anybody could pick up boxes and push them into trucks. Do you want my men or not?' the voice questioned.

Ravi pondered the statement the voice had just uttered; after deliberating for a moment, he responded, 'We'll appreciate every single extra hand we can get here.'

'Good, you'll get '*em*.'

With that, the line went dead, and he was left holding the telephone in his hand.

Ravi turned and tried putting on his best smile and said, 'Well, you see, the HQ might not understand the issues we are facing in the warehouse.'

'I couldn't agree more,' I blurted, 'however, I am sure they are trying to understand. I am here today to talk to you so to understand more. Do you know if HQ intends to purchase a warehouse management system for you?'

Ravi smirked, 'Really? I hope so. It is tough to operate without a system where everything is done manually. But first, they have to sort out the manpower issues.'

Over the years, I have had many chances to observe organisational behaviour concerning warehouse management. When attending sales calls, some bosses like us to visit their warehouses. They want us to provide our opinions on the operations, the people, the processes, and the feasibility of implementing the WMS (Warehouse Management System). They want us to share our observations with them.

I love doing it too, the more I shared, the more I learned.

It was about an hour's drive from the warehouse to the HQ. I took a detour for a famous *Nasi Lemak* (a local Malaysian cuisine dish that given a chance, you must not miss) near the HQ. I had enough time to think through what I wanted to say to the boss. I arrived at the HQ just after the lunch break.

The office was a long rectangular shape, where the boss's office was at the far end, so I had to walk past every cubical. As I was doing so, I heard a yelp.

'Line up in a single line,' barked a voice.

Curiosity stopped me. I looked over to the direction of the voice and saw a dozen men, many of whom had a look of confusion on their faces.

The voice came from a tall, muscular man, in a dark blue long-sleeved shirt that fit snugly to his body.
He was annoyed as he saw his staff moving around sluggishly and talking to each other.

He yelled, commanding them to, 'shut up and stand still!'
Shocked, the men started to settle down.

'As your new boss, I will not tolerate this sort of laziness and insolence that was condoned under the tenure of your previous supervisor, which resulted in a great dip in productivity.'

He paused for a moment for his words to sink in, but the unconvinced looks were visible on all the faces in front of him. 'As a result of that, I've decided to implement a new system of motivation to tackle this problem.'

The men started looking at each other and found similar confused expressions all around.

The muscular man in the tight-fitting shirt continued his rant, 'Each of you has been referred to me by your superiors as the most underperforming person in your respective departments. Luckily for me, and unfortunately for all of you, you'll be the perfect scapegoats for this new regime.'

It was clear to me by now that he was the man Ravi was talking to, especially since he used the word 'scapegoat'.

The people he was addressing began to murmur.

'Mean we salary up?' one of them asked and laughed.
'We change job? Work here now? Feed goats now?' the other asked.
'New gym? Me like feed goats in the new gym. Good!' Another said, mistaking regime for the gym.
'We go gym, we strong like you. Me like you new boss.' Another exclaimed.

I stood there, watching in awe. The labour workforce in the country was mostly imported from overseas and straightforward English would be the most effective way to communicate with them.

'What? No!' the muscular man shouted. Then with a smirk curling at the corner of his mouth, he said, 'All of you have grown lazy as you cool your heads under the surplus air conditioning units servicing this building, all of you need to learn the importance of hard work. With your substandard performance, the punishment that will be bestowed on all of you will be sending you to work in the company's warehouse.'

I had heard enough. I doubted that any of the men would understand or care about such punishment. They were underperforming for many reasons and hardworking was not one of them. By sending the worst employees to the warehouse, it was not the employees that would be punished. It was the employer that would be punished.

A few men burst into fits of laughter as the muscular man put on a stern look. I walked away and towards the boss's office, letting the laughter fade away.

'It won't work, and it will make matters worse,' I remembered that was the feedback I gave to the business owner, Mr Tan, aka the boss.

I also advised him to only implement the warehouse management software after the warehouse operation was stable.

'Is this project too small for you?' Mr Tan asked.

'No sir, no project is too small for me. You have a sizeable warehouse and a prominent home-grown brand, and I would love to associate our company with yours.' I needed to handle the situation with care. I had an experience once where a prospect thought that I looked down on her, and I was only made to know that many years later. That would be a story I would like to share another time.

'The implementation of the warehouse requires the warehouse operation team to spend quality time with us. During the implementation, your operation team and our consultants have to meet regularly for detailed discussions, and your team will still need to perform their daily warehouse operations at the same time. They will be very busy even if the operation is stable. So, you can imagine if the operation is not stable, your team will be too busy resolving warehouse operation issues and will not have time for us.' I explained.

'After visiting the warehouse, you don't think the warehouse operation is stable?' he asked.

'After knowing that the underperforming employees will be sent to the warehouse, I am sure the warehouse operation will worsen,' I answered.

He looked puzzled, perhaps sending the underperforming employees to the warehouse was a tradition for him. After my warehouse visit, there were so many things I wished to share with him, but I knew I could only choose one that he would be interested in hearing, and would help him the most. I needed to pick carefully and choose the words wisely, so I said, 'You are in the trading business *ya*? So, let's say you buy a thermal flask at 20 dollars, get the product shipped to you, repack it, perhaps added some accessories and then you sell at 40 dollars, ya?'

He straightened his pose as a gesture for me to continue. 'Let's say one of your competitors is also selling similar thermal flasks, their brand is as strong as yours. Do you think your competitor will be buying at a much lower price than you?'

Mr Tan shook his head slightly and displayed a confident smile on his face, and he was sure that he had the best price.

'How about if your competitor is getting the flask at about the same price as you? 19.9 dollars or 20.1 dollars?' I asked.
'That's possible.' He replied.

I posted the next question: 'Ok. Let's look at the selling price. Do you think you can sell at a price much higher than your competitor? Can you sell at 40 dollars while your competitor only sells at 30 dollars?'

He gave me a silly look and said: 'Nobody will buy.'
'I see. So, your competitor will be selling at about the same price?'

He nodded, 'if our brand strength is about the same, and both products have a similar quality, the selling price will be about the same.'

'So, my question is,' I said slowly, 'if you haven't noticed, you are having the same gross margin as your competitor, both of you buy at about the same price, and sell at about the same price. So, what will make you more successful than your competitors?'

Both his hands joined and balled into a fist, something I observed as his habit when he was deep in thought.

It was simple, and he would have got it by now. If his buying price and selling price were about the same as his competitors, then everything in between the buying and selling would make him more successful than his competitors, and everything 'in between' would be his supply chain.

I wanted to share with him more benefits, both tangibles and intangibles.

'If you can store and send the products at and in the least possible cost and time, and deliver them without mistakes, won't that be your advantage?'

He closed his eyes, gave me a hand gesture to continue.

'If the products are sent without mistakes, you can minimise wrongly sent products being returned to your warehouse, and then you don't have to spend time and effort in processing these returned products and redelivering the correct products. Aren't these cost savings? Isn't this what you want?'

With his eyes still closed, he nodded.

'Pick faster with less manpower and deliver more without mistakes. Minimising the mistakes so you will have fewer complaints from the customers, would this help in your branding? Which department can give you all these advantages in your organisation?'

He did not answer immediately. I did not interrupt him and I let the silence fill the room. I have learnt through my years that silence, when used at the right time, can be a very powerful ally.

After a short moment, he opened his eyes and squinted with a smirk, 'in my warehouse.'

I smiled and said, 'Your warehouse operation is the foundation of your supply chain execution. So why would you want to send all your worst employees there?'

Six months later, Mr Tan bought the WMS from me as he continued to grow his business aggressively. A few years later, his business attracted a multinational company. After months of due diligence and negotiations, Mr Tan sold his company for what he termed the 'dream' price. He told me I was the first person he informed when the deal was completed. I was happy for him and glad that he had made enough money for his retirement.

* * *

You ought to shift your paradigm. Your warehouse is the foundation of your supply chain, fill it with all the smart people.

'Some mistakes will be made along the way. That's good. Because some decisions are being made along the way, we'll find the mistakes. We'll fix them.' -- Steve Jobs

4

THE GREAT WAREHOUSE JAM

'In critical moments, men sometimes see exactly what they wish to see.'

-- *Spock*

While I was just a RELIC there was an event at the warehouse that vividly illustrates what happens if you take your eye off the ball even for just a day.

The warehouse I was to eventually oversee housed over 40,000 pallets of fast-moving consumer products, the majority of which were plucked from the shelves in full cartons. A few orders were large and required us to send full pallets and some orders required us to open the cartons and pick out the inner boxes within but, overall, the operation would ship out around 150,000 cartons daily with a similar volume coming in every day via up to 100 container trucks.

There were over 12,000 different active products or Stock Keeping Units (SKU's) and over 400 people working there on two shifts over 24 hours a day, operating seven days a week. It was a very busy warehouse.

The products were all stored on pallets and stacked on 7-tier racks that went up about 12 metres in height. The majority of the racking was VNA (Very Narrow Aisle) although we also used a lot of drive-in racking and some selective racking. VNA racking is special because it requires specialised MHE (Material Handling Equipment) to carry the pallets up and put them away into the bin locations in the racking.

The aisle width between the racks that the lifting machines had to negotiate was a little over a metre and the forks were manoeuvrable so they could turn to put away a pallet into a bin on the left side or into a bin on the right side. The warehouse had well over 20 such aisles and in order to put the pallets away as well as bring the pallets down to the floor, we had 12 specialised turret trucks.

These were called 'man up trucks' because the truck would raise not just the pallet on the forks but also the driver himself so he would have a clear close-up view when putting pallets away to the bin.

The warehouse had about 30 docks for large container trucks to unload the inbound products. The same docks were used for loading picked outbound products to the smaller delivery trucks.

All the docks were located on one side of the warehouse.

The inbound trucks would reverse in and the products in them would either already be on pallets and require us to simply drag the pallets out using manual hand pallet jacks or the cartons were all loaded onto the floor of the truck taking up every available space in the container and in such cases we would need to hire some labourers to handle the cartons out of the truck and stack them onto wooden pallets.

Unloading a palletised truck would take 30-45 minutes, unloading a floor loaded truck could take up to three hours especially if the cartons were heavy or there were many different SKU's. I remember there was one lady in her forties, and she could unload a floor-loaded 40-foot container on her own in two hours. Fit as a fiddle she was.

Since space was at a premium and it would be easy to mix up products waiting to be put away with products being picked for shipping out, we adopted a shift system whereby from 9am to 5pm we would manage only inbounds. From 6pm to 8am we would manage only outbounds.

There was a mezzanine floor above the docks that gave a splendid view of all the super-tall racking as well as the narrow area between the racking and the docks where people and MHE busied themselves moving products between the trucks and the racked storage area. This was called the staging area because products would be temporarily parked here while waiting for someone to move them to the correct location.

One morning I was on the mezzanine floor watching the products that had been unloaded from the trucks being moved to the aisles feeding the giant VNA turret trucks that would put the products away to the bin locations in the racks. The put away appeared to be a bit slow but, as a mere English instructor, what did I know? I returned to my classes.

Several times that day I peered down from the mezzanine floor viewing area to notice an unusual number of pallets blocking up the staging area and also blocking up the aisles, waiting for the turret trucks to put the products away. The evening arrived and the coaches carrying the night shift teams appeared and hundreds of night shift workers poured out.

The day shift teams hopped onto the vacated coaches to be swept back home into Bangkok. The picklists came out from the printers instructing the night shift workers what products to pick from which bin locations and in what quantity, and dutifully they carried out their work.

Yet there was clearly some problem with where to put the picked products since the staging area floor was becoming crammed with products still waiting to be put away and now also with products to be shipped out.

By 8pm no space at all was available to even walk through the warehouse let alone drive any equipment there. Every available area was covered with products. Outside, container trucks were still waiting to unload and significantly more smaller trucks and pickups were waiting to load up with the next day's deliveries.

The cause of all that backlog was that on that fateful morning, ten VNA turret trucks had all failed and required maintenance. By the afternoon the remaining two turret trucks had also bitten the dust and were inoperable.

However, instead of stopping the unloading of inbound trucks, unloading carried on as normal and products were moved into the warehouse even though there was no space for them on the floor.

It also seems that the day-shift manager did not see any reason to inform the night-shift manager of the MHE problem and just decided to go home.

The night-shift manager didn't bother coming out of his office and checking the warehouse floor, not until it was too late.

The consequence of this was far reaching and quite disastrous. The main warehouse operations manager was away in a meeting on that day and only found out what had happened the following morning at 7am when he came to work. Of the 150,000 cartons that should have been picked and loaded onto the waiting trucks for delivery, virtually none had made it out of the doors because products from the 100 inbound trucks that had been unloaded blocked all the doors.

In many cases it was now impossible to work out what product was newly inbound and what product was supposed to be shipped out. Some of the VNA turret trucks had now been fixed but there wasn't any space to drive them out of the maintenance area.

Top management were now running to the warehouse in a mad panic since every customer was now screaming complaints at them that no products had been delivered. A decision had to be made urgently about what to do. Our third-party transporters were called in and were requested to take all stock that was blocking the dock doors immediately back to their own depots. There was no paperwork, the products were all mixed up, we had no idea what products they were taking, we just had to trust them, we just had to relieve the blockage.

It took several days to get the warehouse flowing again but by then we were already 2–3 days behind with deliveries. For an operation that works 24/7 there is no window to catch up in the event of a delay such as this.

It would take a month for us to catch up.

Supervisors started to call in sick after a week because of the large number of hours they were being asked to work and from the stress. Even I, the English teacher, was asked to supervise the warehouse floor on some nights because they were shorthanded. Major issues occurred because we didn't know where our stocks were, we didn't know which transporters had taken what.

We also had a large number of orders that may have been delivered to customers, but we had no evidence of it because the invoices had all become mixed up.

It cost us hundreds of thousands of dollars in additional track and trace activities and stock loss.

The operations manager worked for a month putting in over 18 hours a day, 7 days a week to fix the problem, but he was never forgiven and eventually left. Two years later I was still negotiating with some of the third-party transporters on fees we had not paid them for taking the stock from our docks on that day. One principal lost complete faith in us and moved to a competitor distributor.

The distribution business does not treat well those who take their eye off the ball. However, it is from situations like this that I learnt the best lessons, even though in hindsight some of them are obvious.

The key lesson to learn if you are running a warehouse is to walk the floor. There will be no major issue to call out 999 times out 1000 but sometimes you may avert a career-ending disaster.

Always hire managers who are good, keen communicators: people who will update you on everything, no matter how insignificant. You need your managers to be worriers.

When disaster strikes, especially through incompetence and 400 people just not thinking (or, like me, not considering it to be their job, or feeling that no one will listen to them anyway), try not to lose your temper and scream profanities at everyone (Australians in particular should take note since they are seasoned swearers).

It's a stressful time and having your boss swear at you, remarkably does not help to alleviate the stress or motivate you to work harder, especially if you are already working 18 hours a day, 7 days a week. When you need all hands on deck, it doesn't make sense to risk offending some of those hands to the extent that they immediately quit and walk out.

Another cool learning I got was that people lie. Customers lie about receiving products, transport companies lie about losing or damaging goods. Of course, you are thinking that I am so naïve as to imagine that people don't lie; the point here is that people will definitely lie if they know you can't prove otherwise and, of course, if the situation suits them.

On another occasion, in a different decade and a different country, we shipped a huge excess of products to a customer. We only realised a month later and called them up to enquire. They immediately admitted that we had sent too much to them and they were happy for us to take the excess back. It was a rubbish product and wouldn't sell so the customer was paying for storage space and eventually would have to pay to destroy it, so they were very relieved that we took it back.

The final take-away from this is to beware of cost cutting. All commercial operations blame logistics for having high costs and demand that logistics departments find cost savings all the time. Using old equipment that frequently breaks down and trying to cut costs on maintenance is not a smart move if you want your equipment to actually work.

* * *

In logistics and supply chain, if you see something could be wrong, it probably is. Do something about it.

A leadership culture is one where everyone thinks like an owner, a CEO or a managing director. It's one where everyone is entrepreneurial and proactive.
-- Robin Sharma

5

THE BARCODE AFFAIR

> *'The intellect is not all... but its cultivation must come first, or the individual makes errors... wastes time in unprofitable pursuits.'*
>
> *-- Flint*

'You've gotta understand... Surely there has to be another way. This software doesn't work!'

I stood in his small office at the warehouse, listening patiently to him yell. The office was crammed with the excess headcount.
'Surely there must be something you can do...', his voice softened.

Well, it all started nine months ago, when I explained to him the essence of having a barcode imprinted on each of his products.

He had sought my services to come up with a fix for the chink in his warehouse operation. He had a partner in China to manufacture his electronic wares stamped with his beautiful logo, and he imported the products and distributed them locally. The problem was that he needed to know how many of these electronics were available in his warehouse at any given time and to keep an account for every product shipped out of his warehouse to track the warranty period.

The fix was not that difficult. He would be able to record and access each product's serial number upon entry into and exit from his warehouse with our warehouse management software. However, I cautioned him on the effort required to record serial numbers for both receiving and shipping, and suggested he only record serial numbers for products exiting his warehouse.

Buying the software was a significant investment for him, and he wanted the extra guarantee of the ability to speed up his operation by getting barcode scanners to avoid having to input serial numbers manually. It was a smart choice, and I thought his decision would be quick.

But when I visited his warehouse and did a recon on the available products, I found out that none of them came with a barcode.

Providing consultation was part of my services, so I offered him advice that he needed a barcode to be printed on each of his products before running the software. He responded confidently that his product manufacturer in China would ensure each further appliance leaving the factory would be imprinted with a barcode.

It should take between six to nine months to exhaust the warehouse of his current stock without barcodes. So, a waiting period of about three months would be a good time for me to return to kick start the warehouse management software project, and he could use the time to make all necessary arrangements with the manufacturer and to get his team ready for the project.

He agreed.

Three months later, I returned to the warehouse, ready to present the project plan and to start the project.

I felt uneasy when I saw him in his warehouse. I stood there looking at the cartons with the rudest sense of déjà vu assailing me. Did I just step into a time machine and go back three months? Otherwise, why was I staring at all the very same barcode-less cartons?

'Well…the manufacturer in China thought imprinting the barcodes would be quite a hassle. You know, it's err, it's quite a complex process,' he said.

I listened patiently, stunned by his words. Why would it be a complex process for attaching barcodes onto a product for the country that was responsible for the larger percentage of most tech consumed on the entire planet?

Perhaps it was something else? I wasn't sure, but I felt that I was responsible for explaining the importance of barcodes on his products. So, I tried to explain again how essential the barcodes were for the kind of efficiency he had in mind.

He then told me that the manufacturer in China claimed that the barcode implementation would increase the production costs by thirty to fifty per cent, and that was something he couldn't handle, and that he wanted to use the warehouse management system without barcodes on his products.

I told him, of course, he could use the warehouse management system without the barcode, but it would not be too efficient at keeping track of his inventory by serial numbers, and for the accuracy and speediness he required, barcodes and barcode scanners were a necessity.

He disagreed. He insisted his team could handle the system without the barcodes on his products.

I tried to explain again, but he was not convinced.

He then broke the news to me, that he had decided to cancel the order with me, and he had already engaged the services of another consultant and system. The other consultant had told him that everything could be done with additional workers to key in all the serial numbers, and he could get his system ready immediately.

I couldn't convince him otherwise, so I cautioned him on the risk of manually entering all the serial numbers. He didn't listen. As a courtesy, I wished him all the best and politely said, 'should you require any of our assistance in the future, please don't hesitate to contact me again.'

I left the warehouse. I was upset after the meeting, not because I lost the deal. I was angry at myself for not being able to articulate the issues clearly. As a result, he was not able to see that a big disaster was in the making.

Time passed, and in the blink of an eye, it was six months later.

I did not expect to receive a call from him again. From the very first word of a request to fix a meeting immediately, I had a feeling that he was in a lot of trouble.

So here I was, standing in his warehouse, listening to him shouting, 'this software doesn't work!'

'You know, I didn't throw all of your advice away.' He said with an apologetic tone.

I didn't know how to respond. He told me he had hired an extra five hands. From where I was standing there were too many people milling about the place where before there was just a trickle.

So, if the business wasn't moving any faster, then someone was doing something very wrong.

I trusted my mathematics. On average, his warehouse shipped out three thousand cartons in a day, and he wanted an eleven-digit serial number. So, six hundred eleven-digit serial numbers were to be entered into the system manually by hand by each person every day. It was not exactly impossible but trying to do this every day for a few days would prove that humans were not machines. Repetitive reading and keying in numbers was the perfect formula for many mistakes.

'I am now fully convinced that your system is the best, and I am very ready to buy from you,' he said.

There were tiny drops of tears in my eyes. I assumed that it must have been a sudden gust of wind carrying dust into them; I could have really cried out loud knowing that my explanation still carried no weight: it had not struck him that the root cause was the missing physical barcodes on his products.

But then, he said something to wake me from my sorrow instantly.

'Huh? Sorry, I didn't quite catch you there. What did you say?'

'I'm saying that you need to give me a major discount,' he said. 'Think of it like a long drawn out negotiation process during which I've sustained some heavy losses.'

I did not ask him how much he wanted. I was sure that he wanted far more than I could afford. I explained patiently to him again on the barcode issue and urged him to talk to the manufacturer quickly, the faster the better so barcodes could be captured by scanning instead of being manually keyed into the system. In the meantime, I advised him not to record any barcodes until he sorted things out with his manufacturer. It was meaningless to have unreliable data.

'But the software doesn't work! It was a lousy software!' he yelled.

That was the last sentence I could remember, and it was also the last time I saw him. Our paths never crossed again after that.

* * *

Actions require determination; be aware that the supply chain is a lot more complicated than printing a barcode on a product.

'The journey of a thousand miles begins with a single step.' -- Lao Tzu

6

ACCIDENTS HAPPEN

*'When the personality of a human is involved,
exact predictions are hazardous.'*

-- Dr McCoy

Accidents happen, especially industrial accidents and in warehouses where you have that heady brew of humans and equipment moving things. Insurance too can be nefariously tricky.

Take for instance the case of a fire in the warehouse that correctly led to the sprinkler system automatically being triggered and the fire being extinguished in double quick time.

We lost millions, not due to the fire damage but due to water damage – fire damage was covered by insurance, water damage was not.

We should have just let the inventory burn!

When you put humans, especially men, in charge of large heavy powerful equipment you are concocting a recipe for disaster.

On one occasion we were using reach trucks, basically forklift trucks that used forks to lift pallets to heights of around 12 metres, equivalent to the height of 7 pallets stacked on top of each other.

Reach trucks reach higher than normal forklifts hence their name

Reach trucks, like forklift trucks, keep the driver at ground level so the driver needs to have very good eyesight to see the pallet he is putting away or picking from the top rack 12 metres above.

In this case, the accident was not due to bad eyesight but over zealousness.

The driver was putting a pallet onto the top rack. The correct procedure is to bring the forks back down to ground level before driving away. In this case the driver accelerated away with the forks still at the top of their reach. It destabilised the whole vehicle causing it to teeter and fall over.

Twelve metres of truck slowly leaned over and fell; the top of the mast crashed with such a thud that the building shook. Everyone ran to see what had happened.

To this day I cannot decide whether we were really unlucky or really lucky.

In this case the reach truck crashed down with the forks at the top of the extended mast 12 metres high and, at this extreme length, the end of the mast landed on a worker's toe.

The big toe.

This poor lady had her toe entirely crushed but with a few more centimetres it could have easily landed on her head and killed her outright. For the insurance it was a cut and dry affair, the worker got the full payout.

In another episode, 80 drive-in racks (2 sides, each side 4 pallets deep and 6 pallets high) suddenly collapsed. A tangled mess of steel and tissue since we were using the racks primarily for toilet rolls and kitchen tissue rolls.

Strangely, no one was near the racking when it collapsed; it just seemed to collapse on its own accord. Consequently, the racking company got the blame and their insurance paid for the damaged racking and products.

However, a detailed review of the CCTV coverage showed 15 minutes before the collapse a forklift had ploughed into the racking causing the entire set-up to shake dangerously. The driver seemed to be holding his breath during the event until the shaking stopped, so he carefully reversed his machine and drove away.

15 minutes later, it collapsed.

Our manager, being a savvy entrepreneur, failed to provide this evidence and the racking company, being less savvy, failed to ask to review the CCTV coverage.

We dodged a bullet!

Shortly after the collapsing racking event, I arrived at the office one morning and walked in to see the transport-office wall completely demolished, furniture mangled and deformed, computers and printers smashed to smithereens and a forklift truck abandoned in the middle of the office.

The driver maintained, under our interrogation, that the forklift's brakes had failed as he was driving around the warehouse (at night thankfully so no one was in the office) and the machine had careened through the transport-office wall and into the office itself.

I could accept the possibility of the brakes failing but, in order to cause such a degree of damage he must have been driving the forklift like a formula one car. We claimed the insurance so ultimately dodged some of the costs of the damage, but the driver lost his job, a bullet he couldn't dodge.

For the remaining equipment drivers, we had come to the conclusion that radical action had to be taken. Given that this was an Asian country with a strong culture of sexist bias we took the worst action possible in the driver team's mind.

We trained women to drive the equipment and started replacing the men with women. It very nearly caused an all-out strike which was averted only when we told the drivers to accept two women into the team or, if they stopped working, we would replace all the men in the team with women.

The driver team reluctantly accepted and we had no more accidents caused by either gender.

Of course, mixing the genders in an operation can sometimes cause problems that few could have foreseen. Take for example the stock loss we were incurring in our inventory.

It got to the point that we secretly installed CCTV cameras in certain aisles, and lo and behold, we caught a chap during the lunch hour surreptitiously opening a condom carton and taking out a single condom.

The man was summoned to the warehouse manager's office where he quickly owned up to stealing the item when shown the irrefutable CCTV video evidence.

However, this was just the tip of the iceberg.

The manager had the presence of mind to interrogate the man further, based on the strangeness of risking his job to steal one condom. It didn't make sense, until he spilled the beans on the prostitution business occurring on the mezzanine floor where members of the female-only labelling teams were earning a little extra cash on the side during lunch hours.

The last of this short litany of warehouse tragedies occurred during a management meeting at the warehouse.

The main meeting room was located on an upper floor with a window looking out onto the main road. We were a busy warehouse and often our yard would be so full that some inbound container trucks would have to park outside on the side of the road before they could enter through our gate.

On this particular day, one trucker had been waiting so long he decided to unhitch his truck from the container at the side of the road and drive away to get some lunch. The management meeting was often full of dull moments, so it was no surprise that one of the managers was gazing out the window.

The moment turned less dull when he suddenly shot out of his seat and called everyone in the meeting to look outside.

We duly did.

The container that had been unhitched from the truck used steel feet and the front to stabilise itself when not attached to the cab. One of the steel feet was not on the road tarmac and was instead on the grassy verge. We all watched helplessly as the steel foot slowly sank into the grass and dirt and the container, full of new products waiting to be unloaded into our warehouse, inexorably leaned and eventually toppled over completely into the drainage ditch.

As it rolled into the ditch it also crashed into the concrete pole carrying the electricity lines and suddenly with a spark of light, with all of us managers watching, all the lights in our building and in the entire industrial park went out.

* * *

Some things that happen are beyond your experience to prevent or control, especially if you're young and at the beginning of your career. My advice is to enjoy them, they are like the fireworks at New Year – loud and bright and awe inspiring. Also, learn from them and try not to repeat later in your career because people will be less forgiving.

'Don't learn safety by accident' -- Jerry Smith

7

THE MOON PROJECT

'Grace a Dieu. Where is the hostile?'
-- Captain Jean-Luc Picard

Every business is unique and because of that their needs for a warehouse management system are different. While companies understandably want to evaluate software systems before making a purchase, many do not know how. Some get entirely lost in the evaluation process, and a few get wholly carried away. Such was the case for a port company that I once tried to do business with.

I was sitting at my desk one afternoon when Bridget walked by and handed me an RFP that had just come in.

'This is from a port company. One of the services they offer is warehouse spaces for customers to store their products. They will then help the customers to distribute the products to the local market.' Bridget said.

'Sounds good,' I said, 'have you read the RFP?'

RFP stands for 'request for proposal'. The port company was inviting us to submit a proposal for a software solution.

'Yes, and I noticed a few unusual requirements,' Bridget replied. She then pointed out a few requirements, such as having GPS within their warehouse and RFID labels for the inventory stored in their warehouse.

'Weird…are they thinking of getting their warehouse operation to apply RFID labels to all their inventory?' I asked.

Bridget shook her head. 'I am not sure, and it is a bit outlandish. I'm going to make a call to get some clarification on this.'

While Bridget was on the call, I placed a call to Clement, the Asia Pacific service director of the warehouse management software I represented. The software was one of the best in the world, and Clement was usually very busy in Shanghai.

I read him some of the top requirements.

'That does sound pretty out there, something unusual,' Clement said.
'I know. I'm thinking of driving there and checking it out in person.' I said.
'Do you want me to come with you? I'd like to see this myself.' Clement said.
'Of course! I think that is an awesome idea,' I replied.

I whispered to myself and smiled, 'How often would you get the service director of the world's best warehouse management software system to attend a sales call with you?'

Bridget returned, frowned and said, 'the project manager doesn't know the details, he suggested going over there for a discussion.'

Back then, RFID was still very new and costly. In addition, to apply RFID tags on each product in a warehouse requires unpacking and repacking activities, an extra cost to the usually-low-margin logistics business. RFID tags are best applied during the manufacturing process. As such, it was an unusual requirement.

I told Bridget that Clement and I would be going and asked her to arrange the meeting within the week. Bridget arranged the meeting for three days later, but she was unable to go with us as she would be on leave for her wedding. She was to marry our colleague, a senior consultant in our company. Their office romance was a well-kept secret. They were such a lovely couple, and I did not know why they had to keep it a secret.

'By the way, the project manager said that their company has set aside a huge budget for this project. They would like to evaluate us as soon as possible,' Bridget said.

I called Clement to let him know, then went back to work. But I kept thinking about those requirements. What were these people thinking? I had to find out for myself.

Three days later, Clement and I left the city early in the morning to drive to the port. We had always worked well together. He's now my business partner, and we've been working together for more than twenty years.

We had to take some long winding roads and back then, there was no smartphone and GPS wasn't widely available. We got lost a few times and had to stop and ask for directions. Despite this setback, we still managed to arrive 15 minutes early.

We were greeted by Mr Raj, who took us to the warehouse. It wasn't very big, didn't have any racking, the inventory was all on the floor, and half of the warehouse was empty. Clement and I just looked at each other. We were both thinking the same thing. The main reason they could operate this way was that their volume was low.

But they had a big vision. Mr Raj said they wanted to challenge the Port of Singapore, which at the time was the busiest port in the world.

'Our goal is to be the number one port in South East Asia within three years.' Mr Raj said again, confirming what we believed to be accurate.

After visiting the warehouse, we never got a chance to see the port because Mr Raj took us right to a meeting room. A few key people were waiting for us, including the CEO. He was a young man, in his early thirties and spoke excellent English.

'I want you to provide all your requirements to these two gentlemen so they can provide an accurate costing for this project,' he said to his staff.

They nodded and began writing things down.

'You all better tell them everything you wish for,' he continued. 'If you miss anything, don't come and ask for more budget. And I will personally come after you for the missing features,' the CEO added.

A simple statement could trigger chaos, and it did. Before we could even clarify the RFP requirements, more requirements came pouring into the discussion, including some that were out of this world for the time.

'Driver database must have standard and unlimited user-defined fields,' someone demanded.
'Your system must be able to auto-detect and correct all human errors,' another person added.
'System must plan and direct drivers for best route based on real-time traffic conditions,' a third person added.

Clement and I decided not to focus on this futuristic artificial intelligence featured wish list. Instead, we focused on the actual requirements and provided our views on what was needed. After spending all morning with them, we discussed our conclusions.

'From everything you've said it would appear you are looking for a complete overhaul of your systems,' I said.

The CEO nodded.

'To break it down, this is what it sounds like you want,' Clement said. 'Warehouse Management System with RFID capability, Transportation Management System, Route Planning System, Yard Management System with GPS capability, and Demand Planning and Forecasting System. Does that sound right?'

The CEO looked at his men and gave them a gesture to answer.

'We also need ERP, enterprise resource planning system,' someone said.

'Also, a freight forwarding system.'
'and also, the asset management system,'
'and don't forget all these systems must have the capability to auto-detect and correct human mistakes.'

For a moment, it felt like invisible bullets shooting all over the place.

Clement and I looked at each other and shrugged. We knew each other so well that we could communicate using our body language. They were asking for the sky, but if they could afford it, we would deliver the sky to them. We both agreed without having to speak.

'Just out of curiosity, how much is your budget?' I asked the CEO.

He then held his head up proudly. 'I have one million approved from the board, but I don't expect we'll even need to use that much.'

'With all due respect, Sir, one million dollars might sound like a lot but this involves a lot of systems, perhaps you might need to consider a budget increase?' Clement said.

The CEO wasn't impressed, and he said: 'Well, I have told you our budget, I suggest you work within it. We have also called in five other vendors.'

In other words, if we could not fit his budget, others would.

'I understand,' I said. 'would you consider reducing the scope on some of the requirements to fit your budget?'

As we got further into the discussion Clement and I began to realise something even worse. It turned out they weren't even referring to the funds in USD but in local currency which at the time equalled only a quarter of a million in USD. That wasn't even enough to purchase all the software licences!

We let them finish talking, then said we would discuss it and get back to them. As we walked out, a man was sitting there waiting to meet with them. He introduced himself as the senior sales director of a famous German software company. Apparently, most of the reputable vendors were being invited for the proposal.

After we got back in the car and started driving back to the city, we discussed our interesting meeting.

'So, how?' Clement asked. If you happen to be in Asia, we use this term a lot.

'I don't think we can submit a proposal,' I said.
'I agree. They want the moon, but they don't have enough budget for it. I wonder how it's going with the German guy?' Clement said.

I shrugged and blurted: 'I don't know, but probably not much better than it did with us. I don't know how they can expect to be competitive like that. It's just not realistic.'

I was right. Later we found out that not only did the German software vendor not submit a bid, neither did any of the other reputable vendors. The project was dead before it even started.

Lucky for the Port of Singapore, they had the chance to remain the busiest port in South East Asia for the next twenty years, and likely to still be so for the coming twenty years.

* * *

To those who may be considering the purchase of a new software system: people can get carried away evaluating software and losing touch with reality, but our past doesn't equal our future. We can all learn from our mistakes and learn from each other.

Great vision must be accompanied by actionable tasks. Performing a reality check to ensure all tasks are reachable within your constraints will bring you one step closer to your vision.

'If there are nine rabbits on the ground, if you want to catch one, just focus on one.' -- Jack Ma

8

THE TRANSPORT MANAGEMENT SYSTEM

' I'm not in the habit of consulting lawyers before I do what needs to be done. You?'
-- *Captain Jean-Luc Picard*

'Yes, we commit to applying a Transport Management System to your operation this year,' said the boss to the client with his dazzling smile of sincerity that he kept in the top drawer of his desk to wear whenever a customer starts to vent their frustrations.

Such a powerful tool the 'smile of sincerity'. It always made the clients walk away with a gleeful skip in their step feeling they had come away a winner. In this case they had.

'We've got no budget for a TMS,' I nonchalantly mentioned to my boss once the client had gone. I always found it best to give him negative news in a nonchalant fashion instead of a serious tone; the serious tone had the effect of putting him on the defensive and when on the defensive he would slip on the smile of sincerity and talk platitudes till I went crazy.

'We'll build a business case for it,' he replied, not without logic – a business case was certainly feasible.

'We're not allowed to make IT CAPEX decisions,' I tossed this ball over to him. CAPEX stands for Capital Expenditure.

'We won't tell the top management,' he batted back. 'We'll disguise it as an operations expense and not a CAPEX and they'll never know.'

Hmmm.....

Transport management systems or TMS's are notoriously difficult to implement on account of the broad number of features available and the large amount of detailed up-to-date master data required to make those features work.

For instance, you could set up a TMS to automate routing. It sounds easy at first: whenever an order comes in you assign it to a truck. Obviously, it should be assigned to a truck planned to visit that particular area, e.g. if the order is for North Bangkok you assign the order to the truck going to North Bangkok and not to the truck going to central Bangkok. How to do this?

You could set up the system to somehow read the customer address but addresses are text fields and people spell place names in a variety of different ways, especially in Asian countries where the place name has been translated phonetically e.g. Sukhumvit Road, Sukumvit Road, Sukumwit Road are all the same road. In addition, Sukumvit Road in Bangkok is one of the longest roads in the world and travels from central Bangkok south all the way to Pattaya then onwards East all the way to Cambodia.

Which truck should this order go in?

A smarter move would be to assign a route code to every customer, and customers in the same area will have the same route code. When a customer order comes in, the master data for that customer will tell you the customer location is in Route 001 which is North Bangkok.

Easy! Except now you have to manually read every customer address and assign a route code. Which of course is what we did. For 5,000 customers.

That was the easy bit.

An order will come into the system and be automatically assigned to a truck for that route. Unfortunately, customers don't always send in orders for next day delivery, sometimes they cunningly plan ahead and send in orders for a week from now. So, we had to only assign those orders that are for next day delivery and put aside future delivery orders without forgetting about them.

I'm of an age where I will sometimes forget to put my trousers on in the morning, so the system has to be pretty clever to remind me about an order from last week that needs to be assigned to a route today.

The other annoying thing about some customers is that they are sometimes ordering a small amount such as one carton and sometimes a large amount such as two pallets of product.

My truck could fill up pretty quickly with large orders and pretty slowly with small orders. So, we needed to measure the volume and weight of the products in each order and when the truck is full in terms of cubic volume or kilogram weight then we will need to add subsequent orders to a new truck for the same route.

Just to make it more complicated, we may have many different types of trucks that have different maximum volume and weight limits. For our project, we actually had only one size of truck. Thankfully!

In logistics we like large orders because the truck will be full, and we then have to visit only a few places to drop off the orders. If all the orders are very small we may end up having 50 orders on one truck which makes it impossible to complete deliveries in a single day with Bangkok traffic – so not only will a truck fill up in terms of cubic volume and weight but also it can be full in terms of number of drops it can make.

Obviously, we want to maximise the truck in terms of volume, weight and drops so a good mix of small orders and large orders would be best.

The transport management system has to be pretty clever to manage all this. We would need to have master data on the sizes and weights of all the different products that are being ordered so we can calculate the volume and weight we plan to put in each truck accurately.

Also, we want a TMS that is smart enough to realise that it has one truck going to North Bangkok with say, 5 large orders in it, and another truck also going to North Bangkok with 15 small orders so we want to try and balance it out by having each truck carry 10 orders each.

Then you have those customers who can be very annoying. For instance, they may place many orders with large quantities on a Monday and fewer orders on a Tuesday. So, on Monday I need 100 trucks and on Tuesday I only need 70 trucks.

If they are my own trucks and my own staff working on them, then I am paying for all the trucks and the staff every day regardless how full they are or whether they are being used at all.

So, on Tuesday, 30 trucks and staff will have nothing to do and I still have to pay for them. Perhaps I could reduce the number of drops on the other 70 trucks to try to make use of all my 100 trucks; it makes it fairer because all staff can benefit from finishing earlier and enjoying an easier day's work and potentially, I can reduce my overtime bill for Tuesday.

Of course, I would then be paying fuel costs for the 30 trucks that I don't really need to pay. What's the most cost-effective solution here?

I know!

I would like the TMS to optimise the number of trucks that should be used on each route every day based on the cost of fuel, maintenance cost, tyre wear, etc. and potential overtime savings. Getting a bit complicated now. An easier solution would be to have a core transport fleet of say, 70 trucks and use more expensive 3rd party trucks for peak days and periods.

So now the TMS needs to assign orders to my trucks and to 3rd party trucks. I would also want my trucks to have the easiest routes with the fewest number of drops. I'm beginning to sound like a kid in a toy shop who wants all the toys.

By now my TMS consultant is clutching his temples trying to work out how to get everything I want programmed into his system.

'Oh! Then we have customers who have requested a specific time for their delivery – for example they are out in the morning and want us to deliver after 2pm but before 6pm when they close. AND! We want the system to automatically work out the sequence of the drops for each truck; don't want the trucks going backwards and forwards up the same road, do we? That would be so inefficient.'

'WAIT! In Bangkok we don't want trucks zig-zagging making deliveries to customers on both sides of the street because so many roads in Bangkok do not allow this and only provide U-turn options every 2–3 km so we need the system to also know which side of the street the customer is on so we can sequence deliveries to one side of the street first, do a U-turn and then do the other side of the street!'

'Can your TMS do that?'

'Certainly, sir, it's a standard feature!' responded the sales guy. '*Aaaaarggghhh!*' is the general response from the programmer.

Of course, we did all these too, downloading information on which side of the street the customer was located from the maps and from the drivers. We tossed in a couple of fun exceptions as well, such as those customers who have an obstruction when entering their yards meaning only small, low trucks can deliver to them and those customers with special requests such as wanting the delivery team to bring an additional copy of the delivery document with them.

We also wanted to know (before we confirmed the routing) the estimated cost per delivery order since sometimes the volume may be such that some trucks are going out badly sub-optimised and the delivery cost is unjustifiably high. We may be able to call some customers and negotiate moving their delivery to the following day in order to maximise truck use and minimise cost.

'AND! I almost forgot! Some customers only trust a particular delivery person so orders from that customer must be assigned to the specific truck with that delivery person on it.'

The TMS programmer starts to put a revolver into his mouth.

I hate implementing TMS's. It can get bloody.

First, we had to find a TMS vendor. There are so many. Some have so many features that even we had no use for them. Some were so expensive like USD1m entry cost and that did not necessarily include all the features that we wanted: additional features would cost extra.

We travelled to several countries in the region searching for the best value TMS. Incredibly we found one in Singapore, very good value – a vendor who was excited to work with us and could provide virtually all the features we wanted. We did the business case and it looked fantastic: Return-On-Investment looked to be just three months.

These things are normally too good to be true.

We had some fortune with us. The business was fairly stable with no big volume peaks through the week, month or even the year. We sold only full cartons and nearly all the cartons were of virtually identical size and weight.

The customers were very much fixed, they rarely moved location, we had very few close down and very few new customers. The products were well established with not many new products coming out. We had fixed lead times to deliver, no urgent orders and an extra day so we could deliver next day or the day after and it would still be judged to be on time.

This was doable.

We signed the contract with the vendor and began the development. We had already prepared most of the master data, so we were able to get into testing within a couple of weeks.

We had prepared well in terms of what we wanted the system to do so we had no last-minute scope creep functionality to add, something the programming consultant very much respected us for. It took no more than a few months and we were ready to go live.

There's always a 'but'. This particular 'but' had nothing to do with the system itself.

In order to pay the vendor for their system and implementation we had to sign a contract. The contract value was such that legally neither myself nor my boss was qualified to sign it. It would have to go to the finance manager, an annoying grumpy fellow who challenged everything.

He immediately rejected the contract without even reading it because it had not been vetted by the company lawyer.

We tested the water with the company lawyer regarding approvals and, being a logical and methodical fellow, he had a list of contractual subjects that would need approval from different departments within the group. For example, the group IT department would need to approve systems on his list that included ERP, WMS, TMS, VMS… the list went on.

I consulted my boss. 'This agreement from the vendor stipulates it is for a TMS. If I send the agreement to the company lawyer, he will send it to group IT, and they will reject it because we are not allowed to make IT capital expenditure decisions.'

My boss removed his smile of sincerity and put on his thinking cap instead.

'How about Distribution Management System? Is DMS on the lawyer's list?' It was not. So, we asked the vendor to change the name of the system in the contract to DMS.

'What's a DMS?' asked the lawyer on the phone after perusing the agreement document. I explained that it was a requirement from our 3rd party principal, yes it was a software system but entirely separate from any other system used within the company.

We used the ERP and WMS of the principal and did not use any of our own company systems with this principal. The principal wished us to put in a minor system for them to help the operation and the principal did not want to pay for it, instead we would receive payment via the normal monthly charging arrangements for which we already had a contract.

I hoped I had spoken sufficient rubbish to bore him and just get his sign off on the contract clauses. The lawyer was made of sterner stuff. 'You need to get group IT approval for any system,' he stated.

'I think you'll find that 'DMS' is not on your list of systems and besides, this will operate completely outside our company network and only within our principal's IT network since it is interfacing with the principal's systems only and there is no interface with our own company system.' That should put it to bed. No impact even within our own network, therefore, nothing to do with our own group IT.

'What's a DMS?' asked the lawyer again.
'Distribution Management System,' I replied.

'What's that?'
'A system to help manage distribution.'

'Sounds like a TMS' said the lawyer. A big 'uh oh!' shuddered through my brain, the lawyer knows a little bit about IT systems, the whole strategy depended on the lawyer being a techno-dinosaur.

'No, definitely not a TMS, it's a DMS, very different,' I assured him.

'Hmmm,' said the lawyer. 'Reading through this contract it seems very much like a TMS. I guess DMS stands for David Mouland System then.' It's never a good sign when a lawyer gets sarcastic.

We went live with TMS with our principal and it worked well, it saved loads of money for both the principal and for our company.

However, two months after going live we still hadn't paid the vendor for their system and they were becoming disconcerted.

The lawyer had sent the agreement to Group IT who immediately knew we had implemented a TMS without telling them, so they very angrily rejected the agreement.

The grumpy Finance manager thought he finally had grounds to put both myself and my boss in the dock.

We were in trouble.

If we didn't pay the vendor then they would sue us, and they would stop supporting the TMS. If the TMS stopped then the principal would be very angry and might well sue our company or terminate the agreement with us and leave.

The only thing we had going for us was evidence that the system was working well and making us good money and that the three-month ROI was on track.

Eventually even the top management had to accept we had done a good job, we had taken a cheap, off the shelf TMS system and implemented it smoothly at great reward to the company.

However, we had failed to follow the correct protocols to get the approvals from Group IT.

They couldn't fire me because it had been successful. They had to sign the vendor agreement otherwise we would be sued, and we would lose the customer. So, the management raised a second agreement between the Group IT head, the Group Logistics head, the Finance Manager and me.

This agreement stated that I would never again implement a TMS for the company for as long as I remained working there. I signed their agreement and they signed mine.

All's well that ends well. *Sort of....*

Two years later and I am no longer reporting to my boss with the smile of sincerity in his top drawer. I am now reporting to the Group Logistics head and he has been forced to conclude that the company must implement a TMS since many of our customers had begun demanding it.

Group IT had spent 12 months analysing all the TMS vendors and doing costs analyses and ROI forecasts. The consensus was to use the exact same vendor software that I had used for my 3rd party principal 'DMS' system two years previously.

Group IT and Group Logistics were looking for the best person to head up this project. This project was about 100 times bigger than the project I had done two years before.

There were 100 times more SKU's and vehicles (of all shapes and sizes), the product sizes ranged from the size of a refrigerator to the size of a screw. There were hundreds of different principals all demanding their own unique exceptions. Add to that a dire lack of detailed master data.

I didn't volunteer for this project. Instead I surreptitiously left the signed contract stipulating that I was never allowed to implement a TMS on behalf of the company on the corner of my desk.

I don't know how the project eventually panned out because several months later I transferred to another country. I do know that they were still trying to implement it about two years later when I quit the company altogether.

Now that was a bullet well dodged.

* * *

This is a story of management deciding to do something (and getting into trouble for it) instead of doing nothing.

According to the internet, Lysa TerKeurst made the quote about 'Not making a decision is still a decision'. Prior to looking this up, I'd never heard of Lysa TerKeurst – sorry Lysa!

A manager's job is to make decisions and often they are not obvious, and in such situations some managers do nothing without realising that doing nothing is still a decision. When you're in a position where you need to make a difficult decision, that's when your values come through. You make decisions based on instinct and your instinct is shaped by your values. If the decision turns out to be a bad one then you can settle your conscience by telling yourself that you made the best decision based on the information known at the time and in line with your values in what you believed was good and honourable i.e. it was the right thing to do.

'Whenever you see a successful business, someone once made a courageous decision.' -- Peter F. Drucker

9

THE MAGNIFICENT Q

'In my experience, communication is a matter of patience, imagination. I would like to believe that these are qualities that we have in sufficient measure.'

-- *Captain Jean-Luc Picard*

We once worked with an international big-box retailer who wanted to set up its operation locally.

Siva was the senior manager for the operation, while Simon and I were his consultants. We helped him to set up the warehouse management system for his warehouse operation.

It was one of the first local operations to have a full-blown flow-through cross-docking service. What this meant was that there would be a lot of big trucks delivering products to the warehouse and on the same day, many smaller trucks would deliver all the just received products to the outlets. At the end of each day, there should be no inventory in the warehouse.

We had a lot of discussion and meetings on how to make the operation faster and more optimised, and the three of us believed that we could set up the system very well for such activities.

However, one of the biggest challenges we had was time. The business had a very aggressive timeline which resulted in cutting short the testing time by half. The operation team didn't have enough time to test all the business scenarios thoroughly.

With the constraints, we had sat down with the Supply Chain Director and came up with a strategy that all of us thought was a smart plan. We wanted to use the first two weeks of the live operations as part of the extended testing and training period.

What this meant was that the orders should be given to the warehouse in a controlled manner. For the first few days of the operation, the volume should be kept to a minimum to allow time for the warehouse operation to be familiar with the process flow and system simultaneously, giving the operation team enough time to train all the new staff. If there were any system issues or changes required, we would have time to look at it too. After that, once everyone was confident, more orders would be added to the operation and we all agreed that the full-blown operation should happen two weeks from the first day of live operation.

So, all of us worked over many weekends to try to get everything covered.

The first day of operation finally came. The first 40-footer truck arrived at 8.30 in the morning on time, followed by the second truck which arrived an hour later. The operation was running smoothly for the first half of the day, four 40-footer trucks in and twelve smaller trucks shipped the just received goods out of the warehouse to the outlets.

Simon was our technical guru, he checked each and every item in the system interface file and confirmed that everything was in order by noon.

We were relieved, and I told Simon to go home to take a nap. He had worked over many weekends and hadn't had enough sleep. I then went out for a late lunch.

When I came back to the warehouse, something was wrong. The warehouse was busy, too busy. I saw a few big 40-footer trucks queueing up in front of the warehouse.

As I walked inside the warehouse, some of the truck drivers start honking, which provided a distinct sign of their impatience.

But how? Why? There were supposed to be only two more trucks left for that day, but four were now queuing at the entrance of the warehouse.

I quickly went to talk to Soma, who had just joined the team as the Operation Manager. He was on the phone when I saw him, and all he could say was: 'System is slow, we are not sure the reasons, can you please get Sifu to look at it quickly?'

Sifu is a Cantonese word for a skilful person or master. The honour that came with it was like a knighthood title bestowed by the Queen. Soma gave that Sifu title to Simon.

Simon didn't get a chance to have a nap. He was called into the warehouse immediately. The server activities had gone very high, and the system was crawling.

More pressure had now built up. The occasional honks had turned into a continuous annoying blare, with the intention that all souls in the warehouse and within a 1000km radius would share the same frustration with the truck drivers. It was not helpful.

Simon needed time to check the issues. We knew that it would take time to investigate, and more time to resolve the issues once identified. We had to make sure that he had a cool head at that time so he could concentrate on troubleshooting, and he should not be distracted by anything else. So we moved Simon into a small room and told him to focus on the most pressing issue which was the server performance.

Nobody was authorised to talk to Simon except Siva, Soma and me. We wanted to shield him from all the noise, physically and psychologically.

Let him focus.

In the next two hours, it was like an open fire field. Phone calls, emails and text messages jammed up all our communication channels at lightning speed. Everyone demanded answers and everyone was shooting. With thousands of bullets flying all over the place in such a short time, even if I could have dissolved into a small drop of water and lain quietly on the floor, I would still have been hit by a hail of bullets. The supply chain manager called each of us to ask the same questions. He called Simon too, but I answered the call, so he spoke to me twice, and asked the same questions twice, and I provided him with the same answers twice, which was 'we don't know the cause yet, we are checking now.' After hearing it, he went on, twice, to warn me about consequences and demanded an immediate fix.

By 5 pm, the supposed to be empty floor was full of products. The smaller trucks were not able to get into the warehouse because of all the big 40-footer trucks jammed up at the entrance.

Then, Simon walked out of the room and said: 'I found out what happened.'

All of us dropped all our calls. Even though the room was just a few feet away, we sprinted into the room and collided with each other.

Simon said calmly and slowly: 'This morning, three orders were rejected by the system.'

Well, if there were a fast-forward button, all of us would have collided into each other again to reach out for it.

'The reason is that in those three orders, there are a few item codes that are not in the system, so the system considered it as an unknown item, and hence rejected the orders.'

Our heads nodded at high speed as if they represented the fast-forward button. Simon must have realised that, so he sped up his explanation.

'At around 1 pm, our warehouse management system received a huge item master file. I think someone dumped the entire item master file onto the system. There are a few million records in that file, so it took up many server resources to process the file, and as a result the system started to slow down.'

Soma asked: 'Why would anyone want to throw a big file into the system in the middle of our first day?'

Simon was calm and steady as he answered: 'I believe it is because of the earlier rejected orders, there are some new item codes in the orders, so instead of just sending those new item codes, someone sent the entire item master.'

'How many unknown item codes were rejected in those orders?' Siva asked.

'Six,' Simon answered.

It was apparent that instead of sending six item codes, someone made a mistake by sending a huge file with a few million records to the warehouse system.

'Can we kill the process in the server so the system can go back to normal speed?' Siva asked.

'Yes, but better not. We don't know how many records have been processed. Once killed, the system will roll back all the records and the rollback process could take up even more time. I think it is best to wait and let the system finish processing the whole file,' Simon answered.

It was at a point of no return and we agreed that we just had to wait, the system would finish processing millions of records, eventually. But none of us knew what the exact wait time was. Simon estimated that it would take at least a few more hours.

So, we told Simon to head back to get some sleep, and he did.

We now knew what caused the system to slow down, but we still didn't understand why a long queue of trucks was waiting at the entrance of the warehouse. We didn't have time to conduct any investigations.

We were glad that other than slow, there was nothing wrong with the system and it was still working. There were too many products on the floor, and the operation team had to work overtime to catch up. The plan was to stop incoming trucks and to focus on delivering all the products lying on the floor.

We stayed in the warehouse until the next day. The rare occasion provided a unique experience in a silent warehouse past midnight, but it was not for the timid. It was so quiet that at a distance, I could hear workers whispering to each other that the warehouse was built on an old deserted cemetery and creepy stories about a red cloth still hanging on a lonely dead tree a few feet away from the warehouse.

Heck! If I had to go, I would still have to go alone. I meant to the loo.

The system eventually finished processing all the records at around 4 am. Simon reached the warehouse at 7 am and, for the next few days, we took turns to stay overnight to help.

We then found out that on the first day, the business was so happy with the morning operation, one manager was so confident that he decided to ramp up the operation immediately and unilaterally without informing anyone, including the Supply Chain Manager and director. With his instruction, an additional eight 40-footer trucks as well as the two remaining trucks arrived at the warehouse. We were later told that the decision was made early in the morning after the first delivery was successfully received into the warehouse. No one from the warehouse was informed of such a decision. We also suspected that he was also the person who instructed someone to send the huge item master file to the warehouse management system so that the new items delivered by the extra trucks could be processed in the warehouse.

For the next two weeks, the warehouse operation had to work overtime because of all the unplanned activities. Many workers were not yet well trained. The extra volume only resulted in more mistakes made by them. The outlets made tons of complaints of wrong items and quantities delivered to them. Well, they would complain about missing quantity, but they would hardly complain about extra quantity wrongly sent to them. So, more resources were needed to reconcile the stock and transactions.

I was told the overtime bill for those two weeks went through a few roofs.

Six weeks later, everything had finally stabilised and reached its full potential. The operation was able to handle more volume than expected. We had a small celebration in a very small but cosy Chinese restaurant, and we all knew that this success would be remembered for years. The only thing missing was the manager who unilaterally ramped up the operation on the first day. He didn't join our celebration. We were told that it was his last day at work.

* * *

Great teamwork results in great achievements. We all know how important it is to communicate with each other but such communications in projects are often neglected.

'Victorious warriors win first and then go to war, while defeated warriors go to war first and then seek to win.' -- Sun Tzu

10

HAVING A BAD DAY

> *'It would be most interesting to impress your memory engrams on a computer, Doctor. The resulting torrential flood of illogic would be most entertaining.'*
>
> -- *Spock*

Sometimes working in supply chain feels like a thankless job.

I suspect everyone's job feels like that at times. As a logistics provider you are often caught in a triangle between the principal who wants you to deliver faster but doesn't want to pay for it, salesmen needing to hit their targets on the last day of the month so are pushing customers hard to buy inventory in large quantities that they don't want, and the customers themselves who are having their own bad day and are just looking for a reason to complain.

It all lends itself to a perfect storm and the touch point of all these frustrated people is the logistics service.

The principal will complain that logistics is too expensive, uses too many people and has too many trucks not operated properly, so they must cut, cut, cut to reduce costs.

Sales will take more than 50% of the month's customer orders in the last week of the month as they do the final push to hit their sales targets, the consequence of which is that the logistics department needs to have enough people and trucks to pick the products from the warehouse and deliver more than half the month's orders in just one week.

It should be noted that the logical impact of loading the inventory into the market in the last week of the month is that the customers tend not to order very much for the next two to three weeks because they are already overloaded with stock so the whole month-end rush to hit targets repeats every month ad infinitum.

The customers are frustrated and annoyed by the persistent continual visits and phone calls from salespeople begging them to order more in the last week of the month.

The only way to get these annoying salespeople to stop bothering them is to order something. The logistics department, that has been ordered to cut, cut, cut people and trucks, suddenly finds itself requiring double the number of people in order to pick the goods out of the warehouse and double the number of trucks in order to deliver the sudden spike in order volume.

The result tends to be that some orders get delivered late to already irate customers.

The customers take their frustrations out on the delivery people who in most cases are not at fault. At this point it should also be noted that well-educated, articulate people with good social and customer service skills tend not to strive for a career as a delivery person.

The delivery person role is considered a low skilled job which I tend to disagree with. The complexity of documentation (sometimes up to 12 copies of an invoice needs to be signed and stamped by the customer and every customer may have a different number of copies that they need to take as well as poison forms, Certificate of Analysis forms and so on); the complexity of finding the customer's location (some customers expect the delivery people to know that the address on the invoice is not the address they are expected to deliver to); the complexity of finding a legal place to park (different parking laws at different times on every different road in the city that need to be remembered); managing traffic conditions (how many times has a short cut led to getting hopelessly lost or taking twice as long as the normal route?); all this lends itself to a very difficult and highly skilled job requiring knowledge and experience.

A late delivery to an irate customer leads to the customer venting his or her frustration at the poor delivery person. The irate customer will often also bark at the salesperson when he calls next, to complain that the delivery that the salesperson forced on him or her was delivered late!

The salesperson, under pressure from his manager about why he hasn't increased sales, will pass the blame on to the poor delivery service and explain the customer was upset because deliveries are 'always' late.

I say 'always' because one late delivery generally leads to complaints that deliveries are always late even if it was one late delivery out of one hundred. The sales manager will complain to the logistics service manager who will complain to warehouse and to the poor delivery people.

Sometimes the customer will make a complaint to customer service who are at least trained to be polite and professional at all times regardless how badly they are being screamed at.

A good customer service person will investigate and report the root cause of the problem; sometimes however, the complaint goes straight to the warehouse and the poor delivery person.

For the sake of balance there are times, few and far between, when the logistics service and delivery people are rewarded with a thank you from customers and from principals.

There are times when the delivery people really are at fault.

Many times, in fact.

What follows is a short list of the best and the worst in my logistics service experience from customer service to warehouse to delivery:

⚡ **Poorest sign off to a customer complaint by customer service**
'Sorry for your incontinence'. It's good that customer service agents get to know their customers well but possibly getting to know the customer's bowel movements is a little too much.

⚡ **Worst excuse for failing to deliver**
This was in Yangon, Myanmar. I received a call from the operations manager that the road outside the warehouse was flooded and the trucks were unable to leave the warehouse due to the high level of water on the road.

I dutifully informed my boss of this problem, whose internal *bullshitometer* registered a 9.5 out of 10, i.e. he was like a super high-end bullshit detector. My boss told me to ask the ops manager how he had arrived at the warehouse that morning.

'I drove in,' he replied.
'In what?'

'In my car of course!'
'So, you drove your car through the flooded road?'

'Yes' he replied. There was silence on the phone for about ten seconds.

'I will go talk to the truck drivers again,' said the operations manager. Within 30 minutes all the trucks had successfully left the warehouse and started their deliveries.

⚡ Dumbest cold chain delivery

This was another Myanmar classic. Vaccines are normally stored in a 2°C–8°C environment. Healthcare warehouses will often have large rooms that can maintain this specialised temperature.

In order to deliver the products in the same 2°C–8°C environment operations will often use a cold box which is an insulated box with frozen ice packs inside that can maintain the 2°C–8°C temperature for 24 to 48 hours.

The boxes will often have a temperature datalogger that logs the temperature every few minutes and displays the temperature to the customer so that the customer can have the assurance that the vaccine has been in the correct temperature condition throughout the delivery journey.

Vaccines tend to be expensive and any temperature deviation will almost certainly lead to having to write off and destroy the product – at the cost of the logistics service provider.

Our healthcare picker picked a box of vaccines and noticed that the clinic address to deliver to was just down the road.

He decided that since it was close by, he wouldn't bother packing the vaccines into a cold box and instead tossed it into a plastic bag and wandered down the road to deliver it to the doctor.

Naturally, the doctor rejected it because the vaccines were not being delivered in the necessary 2°C–8°C condition, in fact it was 39°C in

Yangon that day.

It cost us over USD2,000.

⚡ Worst trucks

In order to save money, it was decided to purchase our own trucks instead of using a subcontractor for deliveries.

We had a sister company that had around 12 Chinese-made container trucks that they had been struggling to sell for about three years.

Our management decided to buy these trucks since they were really cheap. It was only after sealing the deal, that we discovered once fully loaded, these trucks were unable to climb a hill with a more than 10-degree slope.

All roads out of the city had steep hills so we now had 12 large container trucks that could not carry anything outside the city because they lacked the power to drive uphill.

⚡ Biggest warehouse nuisance

All warehouses will have some method of pest control such as sticky poison bait rat traps, (you don't want your poisoned rats wandering off somewhere in your warehouse and dying where you can't see them), pheromone bait traps (I find this one quite cruel since it arouses the sexual prowess in the male insect and just when he thinks he's in for a good time he's stuck on a glue trap but presumably still aroused), ultraviolet-light, flying-insect traps (even worse since the ultraviolet light is a device used by flying insects for attracting mates but this one zaps and fries the poor horny fellow).

I once worked in a warehouse that stored amongst other things, dog food and cat food. The hardest animal to try to catch in a warehouse is a cat. If it had been a dog it would have been easy since it's easy to make friends with a dog (just whistle, offer food and give him a pat) but cats are far more feral.

It took a dozen guys about three hours crashing through the

warehouse to finally corner the little bugger – several scratches and bites later he was forcefully ejected from the property.

⚡ Trickiest warehouse emergency

Our warehouse manager was a very large fellow, which is good because large fellows can instil fear and discipline into otherwise potentially lazy and unruly warehouse workers.

However, what we didn't know was that he had low blood pressure.

One day, in the middle of the warehouse he suddenly fainted and keeled over. Lying unconscious on the floor, he was so heavy no-one could move him. In the end, probably not the recommended way, we rolled him onto a pallet and used a forklift to deliver him to the waiting ambulance.

⚡ Angriest deliveryman

One of our biggest customers was a large well-known supermarket chain which had hundreds of stores across the country and bought thousands of different products from hundreds of different suppliers to sell in their supermarkets.

They operated their own distribution centre where all these suppliers would deliver the products.

At this distribution centre every product would be labelled with a barcode and then put into a sorting machine. The machine would read the barcode and know which supermarket store the product was destined for and, using conveyor belts, automatically convey the product to the correct loading bay for loading onto a truck that would take it to the correct store.

There was however some complexity, as always.

The barcode labels that were put on the products were related to the original purchase order made by the individual supermarket. All the purchase orders of each supermarket were centralised, merged together so that a large purchase order could be sent to each supplier.

My warehouse would receive the large purchase order and pick in bulk often full pallets, load onto the truck and ship the products.

Once the truck arrived at the customer's distribution centre, all the products had to be unloaded and sorted by individual purchase order i.e. by orders going to each individual supermarket. Effectively we were delivering hundreds of different supermarket purchase orders covering thousands of different products in bulk on big 40-foot container trucks, but we only had the one combined order.

The poor delivery guy had to unload the truck into a small dock space then root about to find each individual product ordered by each supermarket so that the correct barcode label could be put on the carton and the machine could then convey the carton to the correct bay.

One mistake and the entire shipment would be rejected.

Deliveries were routinely made to the distribution centre between the hours of midnight and 4am. The delivery in question arrived at midnight and the delivery guy unloaded his truck of all the products which took an hour. He then rooted around finding all the products associated with each of the over 100 store purchase orders which took another two hours.

It was then found that one item had been picked incorrectly.

Everything was rejected.

The delivery guy remonstrated with the receiving person, but the receiving person was adamant. 'Load everything back into your truck and take it back!' he said.

The delivery guy was apoplectic with rage and he completely lost his head. He grabbed every carton and furiously threw every carton into the 40-foot container.

When it had been originally loaded, everything was neatly arranged on pallets so tossing everything into the back of the container box by box quickly filled the container but there was still stock left lying on the dock.

This only enraged the delivery guy further and he punched and kicked the products to force the remaining items into the truck and finally forced the doors closed.

At 7am I was called to the dock of my warehouse to find the truck returned from the supermarket chain DC (Distribution Centre) and the delivery guy screaming with rage.

The doors of the truck opened and a torrent of smashed dented cartons of product crashed out onto my dock.

Virtually every carton was damaged, and everything had to be written off – including the angry delivery guy.

* * *

It was a Rudyard Kipling poem that talked about 'If you can keep your head when all about you are losing theirs…'

But how does one keep one's head in such situations?

My advice is to search for the logic in the actions of others because, no matter how mad or insane their actions appear to be, there must have been some element of logic involved that made them choose the course of action that they did.

Having an understanding of the root cause of chaos can help you work out how to fix it and prevent it from happening again, as well as how to explain it to your boss.

'Staying cool and keeping your mind calm always pays off for the better.' -- *Penelope Holmes*

11

THE BIG WAREHOUSE

> *'I am pleased to see that we have differences. May we together become greater than the sum of both of us.'*
>
> *-- Surak*

'If you mess up the branch operations, whose fault is that?' The CEO asked.

We had just won the WMS (Warehouse Management System contract with the largest local hypermarket chain. We were to meet with the CEO one morning. We arrived early, so the IT director invited us to join the meeting, and we quietly walked into the meeting room and sat in the last row.

That was the first sentence I heard from the CEO.

He looked at the crowd of about 50 branch managers and waited for a few seconds. Everyone was displaying the best quality of a typical Malaysian, all were very shy, and nobody answered his question.

The CEO then walked to one of the managers, and asked: 'if you mess up the branch operations, whose fault is that?'

That branch manager answered, 'it depends on what type of mess up...'

The CEO smiled, a charming smile that commands attention, and responded: 'Nope, wrong answer.'

He then walked to a few other branch managers, asked the same question.

'It could be the operators working there.'
'Maybe it is the transporters who deliver the wrong products.'
'It could be the security guards.'

The CEO continued to ask the same question to a different person until a brave person finally answered that 'It should be my fault as I am the branch manager.'

He seemed happy with the answer, but then he said, 'No, it is not your fault.'

The CEO did not have a loud voice, he spoke softly, but with authority. He said: 'If you mess up the branch operations, it is not your fault, it is my fault.'

The room turned silent, with 50 puzzled faces. Then he continued, 'because I hired you!'

Well, you can imagine the unvoiced pressures the project team felt when we were implementing the warehouse management system for the distribution centre. We possessed the highest level of commitment to making sure that the project would be a success: we could not let the CEO down, we could not let it be 'his fault'.

We pulled together a solid project team. We had all the key IT people from the hypermarket chain. We had Yusman, the principal consultant for the software; Simon was our technical guru, and Clement and I were both heavily involved in the project.

We had many meetings with the top management, and they were all very hands-on in the operations. They started from a less than 2,000 square feet *Kedai Runcit* (a Malay word for a small grocery shop), and they grew it to a 1 billion Ringgit business. They knew every aspect of the operation so well and we had a lot to learn from them. They listened to us, challenged some of our ideas, but once they agreed, they gave us their full support, which was one of the critical success factors in this project.

Once we got the support from the top management, we had to work on the warehouse team, and we would need their support too. They were first-time WMS users, so they had many concerns. Among those concerns were whether they would still have their job after the system implementation. We knew we needed to address all those concerns to minimise the resistance.

The truth was that the warehouse operation efficiencies would be increased after the implementation of the WMS; the same manpower could be used to handle a bigger volume, and if there were any changes, it would be at a gradual pace. We told the operation team that the hypermarket was expanding the business, so the reduced manpower could be used in the same warehouse as the volume would increase, or they would be transferred to the new hypermarkets. We also explained that the newly acquired WMS skill would be an added advantage for all of them, and it would make their resumes look good.

We were thankful that the supervisors of the warehouse, Rakesh and Ra, were very supportive of the project. They were so excited about learning new skills and, once they found out that their management had invested in one of the best WMS in the world, they were so grateful that they were on the project.

They attended all the training sessions, and then they ran all subsequent training sessions to all the operators; they were hungry for new knowledge, and learned very fast.

They even asked if they could wear office attire, long sleeves and pants, in the warehouse. The approval of this request gave an enormous boost to their morale.

The distribution centre was a 300,000 square-foot warehouse, with four vertical pallet racking positions. The whole top rack was a mezzanine floor, which gave an additional 250,000 square-foot floor location. If someone decided to play hide and seek with you inside this warehouse, the person who hid would win.

There were 438 workers in the warehouse, and yet a person could go inside the warehouse and magically disappear until it was time to go home. One of the extra tasks for Rakesh and Ra was to prevent that magic. They came up with a simple strategy, which was not to catch everyone, just that one unlucky person who performed such magic.

So, they arranged the training sessions and published the training schedule. Every day, the training classes would start at 10am to 12.30pm and 2.30pm to 5pm. They ran the training for a few days, following the schedule to the dot, so all the workers thought that from 10am to 5pm, neither Rakesh nor Ra would have time to walk the warehouse.

That was how one lazy soul who slept in a quiet corner on the mezzanine floor, with a table fan cooling him off, was caught. He was dismissed immediately – but not quietly.

Ra and Rakesh said: 'You just need to catch one person and make sure everyone knows that you can catch them, and the magic will disappear immediately.' So, it did, and since the incident, we never again heard of anyone who dared to mess around with Ra and Rakesh.

After six months of preparation, we were ready to go live.

It gave us a sense of security when the IT director was with us in the warehouse. At more than 190cm tall and double the size of me, it helped a lot when we had to face all the muscular workers in the warehouse. With Ra and Rakesh next to us, both equally muscular if not more, we felt really secure when the WMS went live.

As software consultants, we could not, and should not, command the warehouse workers. Instead, we got help from others who could command them, and in the process, we trained up both the commanders and the workers.

The first few days were the most crucial moments for the project when the distribution centre operation started to use the system. No matter how many testing and training sessions had been held, there were bound to be teething issues, and therefore it was vital to have consultants on standby onsite. It was part of our implementation policy that when all systems go-live, which usually happened over a weekend, our consultants had to be onsite in the warehouse.

We had an incident when one picker intentionally did not follow the instruction given by the system. He picked up thirty cartons of coke from the location he felt most convenient to him, which was the location next to where he stood. He completely ignored the instruction from the system.

It was an old habit. He used to pick goods from wherever he liked as the first-expired-first-out (FEFO) rotation could not be measured. So, he picked up all thirty cartons of coke next to him, scanned the 2D barcode sticker beside the location, and was unable to proceed further.

He scanned the barcodes a few more times, looked around in a blur and then he looked up and murmured a few words to himself, either praying or cursing. From afar, we could see that he was wholly lost, and we had set up a team to explore and seek out such lost souls proactively.

'What is the problem?' asked Ra as he approached the picker, accompanied by Yusman.

'System got problems, cannot use,' said the picker.

Ra held up the training folder, pointed out him the exact page on the user guide. The picker finally yielded and promised that he would obey the system. He then had to put back all the thirty cartons of coke which he had just picked and walk to the correct location to pick up another thirty cartons of coke. That was hard work, but he surely had learned his lesson.

Yusman told me he had counted the exact number of comments of 'system got problems' to be 98 on the first day. We did a small secret celebration as we had expected more.

There was another incident where the warehouse clerk complained that he did not receive an order created by the buyer. This complaint came after the one submitted by one of the hypermarkets about not receiving some products from the warehouse.

In the supply chain, the complaint chain is a by-product.

The IT team, Simon and his team, had done abundant integration testing, and they were confident and comfortable in their work. But they were very cautious and did not comment on the complaint until they had done a thorough check on all the system logs.

It turned out that all these new products had on-hold status, pending action from the quality assurance team, so the products had not yet been sent to any of the hypermarket branches. The IT team also displayed the creation time of the order, the interface time, the time the new products were received, and how long they were being put on hold and by whom.

Astonished, the clerk blurted: 'Oh…you mean the WMS can know so detailed information, *ah*?'

'No, WMS know more than this!' Rakesh and Ra answered at the same time: voice, volume and tone perfectly synchronised.

Rakesh once suggested telling the operation team that the system was capable of catching lies, but we thought that would be too much of an exaggeration. However, I must confess that we did not stop him from communicating such to the operations team.

The IT Director and his team were not just IT savvy but operationally sound, and both Rakesh and Ra respected them. That was another critical success factor. In the warehouse management system, the buck stopped at the IT director. He might not have a soft voice like the CEO, but he could command the same authority. So, if anyone were to talk to him, he had better have his facts straight and no 'trash talk', for he had a very robust left brain that could detect and smell logic fraud from a thousand miles away. But if you had your facts correct, his right brain could provide valuable guidance so that you would end up spending productive time on what could be done rather than what could not.

As a result, this was one of the few projects where bullet-dodging was not required. The project team just needed to focus on their work, and it was fruitful.

The warehouse operation stabilised within one month after the WMS went live. We knew that behind the scenes, the entire hypermarket top management gave us a lending hand. The approach of treating us as their business partner instead of just another vendor was another critical success factor.

* * *

Everything is connected – your suppliers, your vendors, the delivery people, your staff and your customers. Establishing a culture of gratitude is a smart move.

'Our success has really been based on partnerships from the very beginning.'
-- Bill Gates

12

MR CURRENT SITUATION

'But one man can change the present!'
-- Captain James T. Kirk

I officially took over a brand new 10,000sqm consumer products warehouse operation in Yangon, Myanmar on Apr 1. I knew I was tempting fate starting on April Fool's Day.

It was a new country, a new language and a new culture. It also included a Healthcare Warehouse that was too small, so we had to build a new one. Due to poor country infrastructure it was often a very slow process to get products from one end of a very long country to the other, so I inherited several hubs dotted about in various hard-to-get-to locations. So hard to get to, the only efficient way of visiting them was by plane.

Myanmar domestic airlines consisted of small 20–30 passenger turbo-prop planes landing in remote airports often in mountainous areas, sometimes with only one turbo-prop engine still functioning. Finally, in addition, we had to implement a new ERP (Enterprise Resource Planning) for sales ordering, materials management, finance and controlling and including a Warehouse Management System (I think it was called Sad After Purchase from some fringe German software company or something like that).

Implementing such a project is always hard but implementing into a country that previously had been closed and isolated for 60 years and only recently opened up to the world made it even more challenging.

To begin with I had to explain what a WMS (Warehouse Management System) was and why it would be helpful.

With a tight implementation timeline, I had to quickly choose my WMS team from an operation with which I was entirely unfamiliar. They would have to join the other department teams for the blueprinting system design discussions, the master data preparation, UAT (User Acceptance Test) and the actual go live implementation. It required key people, meaning the best staff would have to be pulled from the operation and their time completely dedicated to designing and setting up the new system. It would leave the operations staff very thin on knowledgeable people and leadership for at least six months while these key staff were working on the project.

Our story, however, is not about the system implementation project. Our story began on April Fool's Day, but it wasn't until a month after it began that I became aware of the irony.

The Yangon consumer goods operation operated around 15 trucks to deliver orders around the city. The set up was an impressively logical one. Salespeople would visit customers in specific areas of Yangon and orders would be created that day. The warehouse would pick the orders the next day. The day after, the orders would be loaded onto the trucks and delivered to the customers.

The sensible logical part of it that I liked is that we did not deliver everywhere every day; we delivered to specific areas on different days. This way, the trucks made deliveries to smaller areas so were able to visit more customers and make more drops than if they were spread out making deliveries across the whole of the city.

Since Yangon customers mostly were mom and pop stores and small wholesalers (there were just a few modern trade key accounts with central DCs (Distribution Centres), the order sizes were small, from just a few cartons per order to maybe 10–15 cartons per order.

To make each delivery route worthwhile we had to fill the trucks up with products and still be able to complete all the deliveries within the day. If the trucks were delivering across the whole of the city, they would spend too much time driving around and getting stuck in traffic and would only be able to make a few drops per day.

By focusing the delivery routes on a smaller specific area, we could make 15–20 drops a day and we could fill the trucks up in terms of volume. All this would drive down the cost of delivery per order.

For instance, if the cost of a truck and delivery staff per day was 100,000 kyat and we could only deliver five orders (say 50 cartons) per day then the cost per order would be 20,000 kyat (cost per carton would be 2,000 kyat). Our margins would never cover the transport cost.

However, if we kept the area of delivery on any particular day very narrow, we could deliver up to 20 orders a day (say 200 cartons). The cost per order would be 5,000 kyat (cost per carton would be 500 kyat).

In addition to the 15 trucks there was another fleet of 20 cash vans. The cash vans were similar sized trucks that would travel to more remote areas in the city and sell products to small local stores for cash. While the 15 trucks of the main fleet were delivering against a sales order, the cash vans were just trying their luck to sell to small remote shops. The shops generally knew the cash van schedule and would be ready (with some cash) to buy products although normally the volumes would be very small, normally less than a carton.

Some of these cash van customers had been growing over the years and were buying in larger quantities. A decision was made to move these customers from cash van customers to pre-order customers i.e. salespeople would make regular visits to them and take firm orders and those orders would be delivered to the customers on specific days of the week by the main 15 truck fleet. The benefits would be to lock in the customer and lock in minimum order sizes with them and we could increase the operation of the 15 trucks.

All very logical and reasonable so far.

With the benefit of hindsight, it is easy to work out what went wrong. First, it was decided to reduce the cash van fleet by 50%, i.e.

the volume of goods and orders being delivered by 10 cash van trucks would be transferred to the 15-truck fleet. However, no additional trucks or delivery staff were added to the 15-truck fleet, so the workload of each truck was suddenly increased by 66.7% overnight.

Second, there was a profound lack of communication. As the new manager of logistics for the country, no one thought to inform me of this change even though it took effect on the very same day I started. As a consequence, it was impossible for me to know immediately that there was any difference to previous operations days since I had no experience of previous operations days. To compound this, not only was I not informed but also the delivery teams were not informed either.

When I started, my key manager was a local Burmese chap who began every conversation with the words 'Current situation is....'. A typical conversation in those early days went like this.

'It seems very busy in the warehouse, there are lot of products on the floor waiting to be loaded onto trucks but there are no trucks. Why is this?' A typical daily question I would ask.

'Current situation is that the products are for delivery tomorrow, so they have been picked and waiting to load tomorrow.'

'Okay, but looking at the documentation, these products were picked several days ago; if they are to be delivered tomorrow, why are we picking them so early? Why not pick them the day before?'

'Current situation is that the warehouse will pick all orders immediately regardless of when they have to be delivered so we get the best productivity from the staff.'

'I'm looking at these invoices, and the expected delivery date was yesterday. Why is this still on the floor, waiting to be loaded?'

'Current situation with this customer is they requested to delay delivery so the product must wait until the next delivery day to that area.'

'There are products here with no documentation. What are they for?'

'Current situation is these products have just been picked and we will be bringing the invoices over shortly to attach to the products.'

In the first week on the job you tend to trust your managers especially when they speak with the strong immediate conviction of Mr Current Situation.

At the second week of April we were into Thinyan, the Myanmar new year water festival. This was a long 11-day holiday when every business in the country closes, including our warehouse. It is the best time to go back home and visit family so that's what I did. Returning two weeks later, I couldn't help but notice the same products on the floor of the warehouse, still not delivered and some still without any documentation. The only thing that was different was that there was so much more product lying on the floor than before.

'Current situation is we have many orders after the long holiday, so many products on the floor waiting to be delivered.'

'But looking at the invoices, many of these products have expected delivery dates from before the holiday, why haven't they been delivered?'

'Current situation is that many shops closed early for Thinyan and we could not complete the delivery so will deliver after Thinyan.'

Something was starting to smell funny here. It was about to get a real stink on. My second day back after Thinyan and Mr Current Situation was in my office in a panic.

'What seems to be the problem?'
'Current situation is that none of the delivery teams have reported for work this morning.'

'None?' I asked incredulously. 'Have you tried to call them?'
'Current situation is that no one is answering their phone.'

CuRRENT SiTuATioN

'Do you know where they live? Can you go visit them?'
'Current situation is that we don't know exactly where they live.'

The culture in Myanmar, as I was learning on my third week on the job, was that when the staff are disgruntled, they will go on strike but the unique difference to other countries was that they don't tell anyone that they have all gone on strike.

We used coaches to bring staff to the warehouse in the morning and take them home in the evening and it was on these coaches that disgruntled troublemakers would appeal to their colleagues to not come to work the next day and also to turn their phones off.

By lunchtime, some of the delivery team members on strike had broken and had turned their phones on and we had got through to them. By 2pm they were all in the main boardroom, so I went to meet them. It was like being at a deaf-mute convention.

I greeted them all but got zero response. I decided to get personal and went up to each one personally, shook their hand, asked them their names and about their families and did not talk at all about the strike. After completing small talk to all 30+ of the team I asked them what the problem was. Slowly one of them made a comment in Burmese. My supervisor (not Mr Current Situation) translated for me.

'They have too much work,' he said.

'How come? Is it because of the high volumes due to Thinyan festival?'

'No.' They all shook their heads in unison but otherwise were not forthcoming with further information.

'When did this extra workload start?' I asked.

'At the start of the month.'

'How much extra workload was it?'

'Almost double.'

Perplexing! Double the normal workload!

What happened? I turned to Mr Current Situation. 'Why did the workload suddenly double?' I asked him.

He shook his head. 'Current situation is that nothing really changed.'

I turned back to the delivery team. 'Did the number of orders double?'

'Yes.'

'Did the number of customers you had to deliver to double?'

'Yes.'

'Did the number of cartons you have to carry in the trucks double?'

'Yes.'

I turned to Mr Current Situation again. 'Nothing really changed you say. Did anything at all change?'

'Current situation is that we are delivering some orders to cash van customers.'

'Ok, so how many cash van customers is this team now delivering to?'

'Current situation is that about double the number of customers.'

It seems that Mr Current Situation was also using the alias of Mr Economic With the Truth.

Eventually we persuaded the delivery teams to come back to work. We got a third-party transporter to support with additional trucks and staff.

However, the damage was done.

The delivery teams had found that they were unable to physically fit all the ordered products assigned to their trucks each day inside the truck, so each day they had to leave some orders on the dock.

Since they were making double the number of drops each day, they were coming back to the DC around 9pm whereas previously they would be back by 6pm.

They were unable to complete all the deliveries so had to unload undelivered products from the truck and dump the products on the dock floor.

Also, many orders they had tried to deliver had been rejected by customers because the deliveries were being made late. Signed invoices had been lost or mixed up due to the huge number of documents they were suddenly having to manage.

In summary, we did not know what orders had been delivered successfully and what orders had not. We did not know if some products from an order had been rejected or not and we did not know where those rejected products were.

Products rejected, products failed to deliver and products pending to be delivered were all mixed up now on the floor of the warehouse and it was getting more and more crowded and mixed up. Add to that were the huge number of customer complaints and phone calls we were being inundated with.

I met the Country Manager and asked him if he had known about the change of cash van customers to pre-order customers.

He admitted he knew all about it.

I asked him why he didn't think it was important for me to know.

According to him, Mr Current Situation had assured everyone that the transition from cash van sales to pre-order deliveries would be easy and no extra resources would be required. Mr Current Situation was now Mr Man with A Target on His Back.

We had to tidy up and it would not be pleasant.

We had to stop taking orders and stop picking for a few days and the salespeople who had to stop visiting customers were told to go to the warehouse to help.

Warehouse staff isolated the products on the floor, products that we could not work out where they had come from or where they were supposed to go to.

With goods that we knew were to be delivered to customers, we needed to confirm that the customers would accept them before we bothered shipping them since some orders were three weeks late.

If the customer would not accept them, we would have to cancel the invoice and put the goods back into the warehouse. There were hundreds of orders that we did not have any proof of delivery for, so we did a customer survey.

If we asked the customer directly 'did you receive your order?' the chances were the customer would realise there had been a screw-up and would lie to us.

So, we contacted the customers to make a survey on how well we had delivered to them and if there had been any issues with recent deliveries. This way we could understand which orders had been received and which had not. We could then cross reference this back to the huge pile of products that had been segregated.

It was a massive undertaking since we had to continue the business and could not suspend sales for more than a couple of days. We had to reconcile all the old orders and goods and at the same time we were still trying to implement the new computer system.

Many goods had gone missing: either the customers lied about not receiving them or the delivery staff lied about completing the deliveries.

We had a huge stock loss in the stocktake.

Mr Current Situation had taken so much criticism and stress he gave me his resignation. I rejected it and told him the mess had been created by him, now he had to stay on and help clean it up.

Eventually we got back to normal and by that time we were about to go live with our new system. That though is a completely different story.

* * *

Sometimes a new boss will come in and have no trust in the existing staff yet have no real basis for distrusting them.

The result is often that good staff do not feel respected and will leave while bad staff (who were never respected) will suck up to the new manager and potentially get promoted to positions where they can do greater damage.

Alternatively, a new boss can begin by trusting the existing staff and slowly working out the good from the bad. As in this example, trusting the existing staff from the start led to disaster.

However, there is no way to prove leading with distrust would have been any better. 'Give a man enough rope and he will hang himself' is a classic English idiom.

In this case, Mr Current Situation clearly had the trust of the country management, something I had not yet earned.

Consequently, I had to trust him until such time that the country management had lost trust in him i.e. give him plenty of rope to foul up the operation until it was clear he had fouled it up and had metaphorically hung himself.

Well, I think we tried very hard not to be overconfident, because when you get overconfident, that's when something snaps up and bites you.' -- *Neil Armstrong*

13

A GREAT FALL

'You know the greatest danger facing us is ourselves, and irrational fear of the unknown. There is no such thing as the unknown. Only things temporarily hidden, temporarily not understood.'

-- Captain James T. Kirk

Not everything goes according to plan, even though it might be a great plan.

For our first few overseas projects, we offered a steep discount, hence we did not expect to make any profit. We needed a very experienced team to deliver the overseas projects, or we would end up making losses. It was a necessary risk for our business expansion, but to mitigate the risk, our most experienced core team would need to be in charge to deliver the projects.

When we were all busy with the projects overseas, someone needed to take care of the projects in Malaysia. So, I hired three experienced senior consultants to form another team for local projects in Malaysia. We only had two projects in Malaysia at that time, and to be safe, I hired two more junior consultants to be part of the new local team. I felt safe, but I wanted it to be safer.

Knowing that all our core members would be tied up with the overseas projects, I planned a profit-sharing scheme for the new local team to motivate them and get their commitment in ensuring all projects would be successfully delivered.

It was a win-win formula, so I thought. We would make our company so great, a part of my ego emerged.

I trusted my core team, so I extended the same level of trust to the new local team. I subscribed to the mantra of 'if you employ a person, don't doubt him; if you doubt him, don't employ him.'

I made haste and told the new team of my intention, and I felt that I had enough of a safety net built-in, so I put my focus entirely on the overseas projects.

That was the start of an intensive and sleepless fall, a life lesson for me.

After feeling completely safe with putting the local projects into the hands of the new team, we took on a few additional overseas ventures. Some of them were quite complex projects, so it consumed a lot of our time.

One day, I received a resignation email from one of the new team members. It was an unusual email, with his last day of work clearly stated in bold. Usually, after receiving a resignation letter, the human resource person would go through the annual leave records and then notify the person of his last day of work. So the bold words, 31st July, caught my attention since HR had not yet been informed. It was already late June, and our normal notice period was between two and three months. I thought it must be a mistake.

I was overseas at the time, so I did not attend to it immediately.

A week later, I sat down with him in person, trying to understand his reasons for quitting as he was the key person in a local project, and the project had not been completed yet. He told me that he had got an offer for a senior position in an Australian company, which had requested him to attend a two-week training in Europe which would be held in the first two weeks of August.

'This is a rare opportunity, and I hope you can understand,' he said.

'I do, but you are the key person in our project, and the project hasn't gone live yet. Can you let your new employer know about your notice period and the situation? I am sure they will understand,' I implored.

'I have already done so, but there is only one training session each year, so if I miss this one, I have to wait for another year. My new company will buy me out, and they will pay for the short notice period. But don't worry, I have done everything, I have installed the software, I have configured everything, and testing is ongoing. I will complete everything next week, and everything will be smooth. I will finish everything before I go, don't worry,' he said calmly.

Something in his body language told me otherwise. I asked, 'When will the project go live?'

'First of August,' he said, 'but don't worry, I have done everything, and everything will be fine.'

So, Mr Everything-Will-Be-Fine had planned his last day to be one day before the go-live date of the project of which he was in charge. Could it be that he was not confident in his work, so he does not dare face it, and he wanted all the problems to be given to someone else? Would a person who possessed just the tiniest bit of pride or integrity make such a move?

It was clearly a lost cause to try and change his mind, so I did not pursue further. If the person in charge of a project did not take pride in the most important milestone of the project, i.e. the 'go live', then it suggests a low standard in the quality of work, a lack of courage and dignity. Mr Everything-Will-Be-Fine certainly did not have everything completed.

It was a tough situation for us as the project was approaching the go-live date, and we needed to inform the customer that we would be handing the project over to another person. The customer would surely have concerns and make a noise. Added to that there wasn't any other person to hand over to. I had to look for someone.

I told Mr Everything-Will-Be-Fine to hand over all the documentation, the minutes of the meetings, the project structure, project plan, the functional design documents, the test scenarios and test scripts.

'Err...we don't have all these documents, the project is very small, so we didn't have all these,' he said. Mr Everything-Will-Be-Fine did not have anything I asked for.

Not a single document.

If I had a punch bag, I would have stuck his photo on it and focused on poking his eyes and nose with all fingers, and I was very sure about which finger to use most. There was a project process to follow, regardless of whether a project is small or not; his duty was to follow our implementation methodology to produce all those documents which he had not done.

The situation was more alarming than I had thought. A furious customer was in the making and I did not have any solution.

Meanwhile, a few phone calls came in from overseas and more meetings needed our presence. My attention was once again diverted.

A few days later, another complaint came in about another local project. During the go-live of this other project, our senior consultant did not join the project side. Instead, he sent the junior person there, and the go-live was such a mess, the customer threatened to take legal action against us.

Only two projects had been given to the new team, and both had severe issues.

The next day, another senior consultant on the new team hinted that he wanted to resign and demanded a raise.

A few days later, I found out one of them was secretly doing some other business outside the company, and he used my name to get business for himself. This is another story of my own naivete, which I will share another time.

It was now clear, there was no argument: one punch bag was never going to be enough. I had to keep reminding myself not to let my rage take over, or I would have injured all my fingers, and I was sure which finger would have sustained the most injury.

All these issues resulted in an inevitable delay in the projects and any delay in our projects would cost us dearly.

We had overseas projects, which by design would not be profitable, we had local projects that surely would make losses, and while expanding our business overseas, we had incurred many more unexpected expenses.

Our cash flow would soon be a big issue.

I needed to act quickly, I went through our financial reports and spotted one customer who had not paid us for quite some time. I asked our finance for details, and she showed me all her follow-up emails, the last one with the subject 'Outstanding Payment Gentle Reminder #26'.

I gave them a call, and they told me they had a cash flow issue. I wanted to say to them so did I but doing so would only be viewed as an act of extreme sarcasm, so I held back the thought.

The next few months were just a nightmare. Everything I thought would never happen, all happened at the same time.

That customer did not pay us immediately. I had to escalate the matter to their CEO, but our payment still dragged on. I had to call the CEO on a few weekends to chase for payment. One time, he was playing golf, and he got very annoyed.

By the time he finally released the payment to us, our relationship had broken down. I could not preserve it during the process of chasing payment. He also did not pay us in one shot. Instead, he gave us a few post-dated cheques.

In the meantime, the other two customers were furious; they demanded more resources to be put into the project, and one demanded a full refund.

One angry customer called an employee who had left us, and that ex-employee told him that because he did not receive the shared profit, which was promised to him, he left. The customer called me and yelled at me, lecturing me that I should not have broken the promise.

What profit?

I felt that it was pointless to try and explain that we had not made any profit to share, that was the result of my melancholy for the whole situation I was in. I simply did not feel like explaining, so I did not bother, I just kept quiet and pushed the noise aside.

Why would these ex-employees expect profit sharing when they failed to complete the projects?

Maybe it was just their mindset. Maybe they could not comprehend the value of a business when they had not endured the risks and hardship in building it. It's possible that some people take their job for granted and are unable to handle the opportunities and mistakes when confronted with them; through fear or lack of self-assurance they take actions that are potentially less than wise. Perhaps in some people's minds, bosses need not actually do any work, so they behave accordingly without knowing that in reality, all the best bosses work the hardest.

One ex-employee even told our customers that our entire core team had left us which was blatantly untrue. One of our competitors said to some of our customers that we were about to wind up. A few customers believed them and terminated our support services.

By now, all the invisible bullets were flying, each one bigger than the previous, but I continued to keep quiet and ignore all these noises. I pushed all the negative news aside and chose not to be affected by it. I needed my focus.

My stress was at its peak, and our cash was running low.

An entrepreneur's life can be a very lonely journey. All this stress was only known to me. I kept it a secret, and I slept with my eyes open for many nights. Every day, my tired eyes were red. I did not want to let anyone worry. I wanted our core team to concentrate on what they were best at.

'Am I going to fail big time?' I questioned myself. I refused to fail, but the famous Star Trek quote 'resistance is futile!' kept popping into my mind. For so many sleepless nights, I felt helpless.

Albert Einstein once said that two things are infinite: the universe and human stupidity, and he was not sure about the universe. He was referring to me. I had been so foolish to have created this situation. As a result, it was only fair for me and only me to bear the stress.

It was the darkest period of my entrepreneurial journey. If I didn't have a strong positive mind and a firm belief in our team and myself, I would have fallen.

There were only two options left. One was to cut the losses, stop our operation immediately, and take out all the remaining cash. With the money in hand, we could set up another business.

It was logical and it was an easy way out, but what about our existing customers who had bought our software and services?

What would I become if I let them down like this?

The other option was a difficult one: it was to find ways to deliver the projects, and in the process, take on the real risk of losing everything I had, all with the knowledge that the customers would never learn to appreciate any of it.

I didn't like to do easy things, or perhaps I was just conceited.

'Just do it,' I said to myself. There was no logical explanation for my decision.

I took out all my savings and pumped it into the business. I remembered there was a time when I survived a week with only 10 dollars in my pocket. Nobody knew, and nobody should have known. I didn't allow my faults to have any impact on our employees. There was no pay cut. Business as usual.

I did not plan for anything else. There was no plan B and I just wanted to make it work. It was an insane and impulsive move. I did not know what the outcome would be. I did not know if the customers would eventually understand and appreciate it. I just wanted our team to do their best in bringing the projects to success.

I wanted the right closure of the projects.

The core team found many issues in the local projects and among them was the manual manipulation of the test results. Instead of applying software patches, the ex-employee had gone into the database and changed the data, so as to make it look like the test had produced the correct result.

It also turned out that there was no training in Europe and it was not an Australian company that Mr Everything-Will-Be-Fine had joined. His new boss's boss knew me, and we bumped into each other at a social gathering, and we talked about it. I didn't know what happened after that, and I didn't care.

A company is not a place or a piece of registration paper. It is the people. We did a clean up, we quickly let go of a few more employees and started to rehire slowly.

I was very grateful that we had a reliable and committed team. We stood tall in the most forceful storm, we did not let the chill wind blow us apart, we did not let the rain pierce our souls, we did not break down, and we didn't let ourselves down. We trusted each other, and our passion guided us to the light that shone through the darkest of times.

Everything happened for a reason; all the sufferings were to get us ready for something bigger.

We became stronger after the setback. We had made it known to our customers that no matter what, we would deliver our promises. Soon after, we won a few big projects, each bigger than the previous one. We had expanded our business to more places and we grew our company to a much bigger size.

We won a global project award with one of our customers, and I was told we were the first Asian company to have obtained such an honour.

* * *

A harrowing but great lesson for me. Trust needs to be earned, it will not just be given. Until it is proven, I will never leave the business in the hands of those who have not earned it.

Everyone makes mistakes. Learn from your mistakes, it will make you wiser.

'The key to success is failures.' -- Michael Jordan

14

THE WALL

*'There is a way out of every box, a solution to
every puzzle; it's just a matter of finding it.'*
-- *Captain Jean Luc Picard*

Marathon runners often talk about the wall. When they face exhaustion
and self-doubt it appears as a wall before them, insurmountable. The
wall is the ultimate reason to give up and go home.

Back in Myanmar we had gone live with our new ERP (Enterprise
Resource Planning) and WMS (Warehouse Management System).

It had been a bumpy ride.

In the first place, the staff were not familiar with the system. There
were project ploys set up to try and deal with this issue because it was
one that cropped up time and again on virtually every new system
implementation. Our ploy was to do a staff stress test.

It meant bringing in all the staff from all departments on Sunday
and giving them an actual full day of transactions to key into the test
system and to test their own proficiency. If they were able to key in all
the transactions by 5pm for an actual day, then they were ready to go
live.

Probably.

You can never simulate a real operations day on a Sunday because on a real operations day the staff on the warehouse floor are physically moving pallets and boxes but in our staff stress test we were not moving any products; we just had the system users keying in the receivables, printing all the picklists and confirming them in the system.

Also, on a Sunday, you don't have principals and salespeople calling you every ten minutes. Basically, the stress test should be easier than the real thing. Our warehouse 'super-user' who I had handpicked to lead the warehouse management system project was clearly keen on going live on time, so took it upon himself to ensure the stress test was successful.

During the post-mortem after Go Live we explored why the staff were so unfamiliar with the system even though they had managed to key in a whole day of transactions. We discovered that 90% of all the transactions had been keyed in by one person, my hand-picked super-user who had worked like a demon to key in everything.

Secondly, the consultants did their normal trick of transporting the wrong versions of the programs to the production system. For these projects there are normally at the very least a Test server and a Production server.

Every project has its own unique requirements for Reports, Interfaces, Customisations, Enhancements and Forms. So all these things require consultants to write specific programs to support them.

This RICEF, as it was sometimes referred to, was tested by the users using the system installed in the Test server.

Nearly always the programs don't work as expected so they need to be modified and retested. It's important that the consultants writing these programs have a strong system for keeping track of different versions otherwise they might not know which one is the final version to install on the Production server for Go Live.

In virtually every project I have been involved in, the consultants had installed the wrong versions of the programs in the Production server just before Go Live. The consequence was that all the errors that the users pointed out during testing recurred on the first day of Go Live.

Picture wild-eyed users pulling their hair out, screaming at consultants who counter claimed that the users obviously didn't test properly, leading to a slow dawning in the consultants' brains that they had uploaded the wrong program versions. This inevitably led to quick and quiet uploading of the correct versions followed by users calming down and straightening what hair they had left and the consultants tip-toeing away before they got interrogated on why they uploaded the wrong versions in the first place.

Thirdly we got to the real system bug issues. The first two issues shouldn't really happen but were the result of including humans in any system or process. The third issue always happens, there are only so many situations you can think to test and there are so many more situations in that scary place called 'reality'.

There are always things the system does not consider and cannot cope with and new programming has to be put in place which may take a few days at least.

The trick for coping with this is to not linger on the transaction that is stuck or causing a problem. You have to pass it to the consultants to fix and get on with the other thousands of transactions in the queue otherwise nothing will get done and you will have a massive backlog. It's like standing in the queue at the bank, stuck behind the guy carrying six bags of small change, which will take the bank clerk about an hour to count; and all you want, is to deposit ONE single cheque.

To cut to the chase, all of the above happened in various volumes leading to our bumpy ride at Go Live. By the time it was all fixed and transactions were being created normally, we had a massive backlog of orders. The order tap had finally been turned on full and we were getting flooded.

In the warehouse we had a couple more issues in that my hand picked super-user had failed entirely to train the warehouse staff how to read any of the forms so when we handed over the picking lists to the staff they had no idea what to do with them.

The picking list simply tells the picker what location to walk to in the warehouse, what product to pick from that location and what quantity. Once picked, the picker can tick with a pen that the line has been completed and then go on to the next line.

My pickers were straight off a farm in a country that had been in splendid military isolation for 60 years. It took hours to explain to them and we had to follow them around every day for weeks afterwards to make sure they didn't revert back to just picking whatever they wanted from wherever they wanted.

It took us three weeks to catch up. Staff became more familiar; they had no choice – we were not going to go back to the old system. Programs worked properly, forms printed correctly displaying correct data, reports issued from the system giving useful, accurate information. The bugs were mostly fixed and most importantly the staff had stopped a rabbit-in-the-headlights frozen with fear impression every time they made a mistake, or a transaction failed or had a problem.

In terms of a marathon, I would estimate we had completed around

24 miles of the 26.75-mile course. By the fourth Tuesday since Go Live all was well, operations proceeding, backlog all caught up and no orders pending for more than a day. Time to sigh with relief and have a soothing cup of coffee.

At 5pm, the day almost done, we got the call from IT.

Stop printing all invoices. Stop shipping all orders.

What's up?

Apparently, our IT team had made a change to the invoicing program at the weekend and had transported a new version of the invoicing program to Production without anyone testing it. All the invoices generated on Monday and on Tuesday were wrong.

'*Oops!*' said IT, figuratively.
'Arrange a lynch mob!' I ordered the operations team, half seriously.

Super Hi-tech (SH) IT to the rescue (meant very tongue in cheek), they had to transport the new corrected invoicing program right now and then reprint all the invoices generated up to now. That was about 10,000 invoices. They would send the new invoices to the warehouse to fix the problem. Hardly a rescue. More of a 'drop the bomb off at the warehouse'.

So, on the Wednesday morning, my hand-picked super-user was seated at his tiny desk looking through a box of invoices with dozens of yet unopened boxes of invoices all around him. The problem was ponderous.

- Many invoices had already been shipped to customers on the Monday and Tuesday. These invoices would need to be replaced with the new ones meaning our delivery team would need to visit the customers and beg them to give back the old invoice in exchange for the new one.

- Many invoices had been printed and attached to the products on the floor of the warehouse, but the orders had not yet been shipped. We would need to find the products on the dock floor and their invoices and exchange the old invoices for the new ones.

- Many invoices had been printed but not yet attached to the products in the warehouse. We would need to change those invoices for the new ones before attaching them to the products.

All we had though were boxes and boxes of new invoices in no particular order. Firstly, we would need to classify these new orders into each of the groups described above. My hand-picked super-user was looking at invoices one by one on a one square metre desk, trying to work out if it had already been shipped or was in the warehouse somewhere. Even if he speeded up to spending just 10 minutes per invoice and worked 24 hours a day, it would take 70 days to get through 10,000 invoices.

He must have been at this for a while because his eyes had glazed over, and he seemed barely conscious. I asked him what his plan was, and his response was a zombie grunt *'uuuurrrgggghhh'*. For a moment I though he was going to try and eat my brain. I gently advised him that we needed to take the invoices to the boardroom which had the largest table and bring in additional staff to help go through them.

It was clear he had hit the wall. Saying nothing at all he handed me the invoices that he had stuffed in his hand and walked out of the office.

That was the last I saw of him that day.

I got some staff to carry the boxes to the boardroom. I got the admin lady to run off a report of the invoices already shipped and the orders still in the warehouse. I got a supervisor and a team of about 5 people and had them work on matching the invoices in the boxes to those listed in the reports.

It took three days to work everything out and another week to catch up with all our deliveries due to the delay in shipping that it caused and the extra work the delivery teams had to do to exchange the invoices with the customers. My hand-picked super-user turned up the next day and had no memory of the day before or even of walking out on me leaving me with the mountain of invoices. That is the effect of the wall.

You can't dodge the wall.

* * *

Never dump on someone a task that you are unwilling or unable to do yourself. Assuming someone else will work it all out for you is a recipe for disaster. That also applies to assuming IT will do their job properly as well.

'We cannot solve our problems with the same level of thinking that created them.' -- Albert Einstein

15

THE PEANUT HEAD

'You exceed your own standards for self-preoccupation.'

-- *Captain Jean-Luc Picard*

I looked into the mirror, combed my hair, straightened my shirt and inspected my shoes one last time, to make sure that I looked good for the big day ahead. I had six VIP guests today, all of the top brass from a telco in Thailand.

My customer was an international third-party logistics company, and I was their exclusive software partner where I supplied them the WMS (Warehouse Management System) for all their warehouses in south Asia. The Thai telco was my customer's prospect. My customer was bidding for a large project in Thailand where these six gentlemen came from, and if they won the project, I would be supplying the WMS to their warehouse in Thailand.

The purpose of the visit was to inspect one of my customer's warehouses in Jakarta, which handled a similar telco operation. Should the Thai guests be impressed with the operation, it would boost their chances of securing the deal. I was to walk through the WMS processes with them and answer their questions related to the software. I was comfortable because I knew the details, having been heavily involved in the system implementation.

The negotiations between my customer and the Thai telco company had already begun. It was a massive deal, I was very excited, and if this deal went through smoothly, it could give us a foothold in Thailand and substantially increase our revenue.

I worked very closely with Eldon, who was the Operation Director of the company. He arranged a people carrier, a luxury MPV, for the trip. He felt that if the Thai gentlemen were able to travel in comfort, they would more likely have a good impression of the day overall. They had arrived the night before and had been put up in a hotel.

Following the warehouse visit, the Thai guests were to catch the evening flight back to Bangkok. The entire trip was strictly business and was to be over quickly. As such, everything needed to be executed with precision. One small mistake could have an impact on the whole deal, so the MPV arrangement was very thoughtful and appropriate.

Both Eldon and I wanted the deal, and we conducted a rehearsal of what to present a day before the warehouse visit. We were confident that we could put on a good show. I stayed in the same hotel as our guests, and I would travel with them to the warehouse while Eldon waited for us there.

We started off early in the morning because of the condensed nature of their visit. We met at 7 am in the hotel lobby, and after they had checked out of the hotel, we greeted each other at the hotel's entrance.

I introduced myself to Yut, who was their Supply Chain Director, and I intended to show off and fully utilise my Thai language with our Thai guests.

'Sah wah dee khrap,' I greeted him.

'Sah wah dee khrap and a pleasure to meet you,' he replied with a warm smile while shaking my hand. 'I'm Yut. Thank you for the hotel. The room was very nice, and I had a good sleep.'

'No problem,' I replied, 'Hopefully the car, and then the warehouse visit, will give you the same satisfaction.'

We exchanged business cards, and upon receiving his business card, I said, 'khaawp khun khrap,' which meant 'thank you.'

There, I had just fully unleashed my whole arsenal of the Thai language. I knew only two Thai phrases, and I had just used them fully.

The MPV arrived 10 minutes earlier than the pick-up time, so I gestured towards the car, and our driver welcomed us into the vehicle. Moments later, once everyone had settled in, we were due to set off. However, for reasons unknown, we were still sitting in the car for an extra 15 minutes.

I was not happy. The driver was standing outside the car, and he was on the phone. Why was he on a call when we should be on our way. Why couldn't he drive with a handsfree? Why was he causing a delay?

Well, at least we were comfortable in the car. I was impressed by the interior of the vehicle. It was spacious. Everyone was able to sit next to one another without intruding on each other's personal space. Most importantly, it was cool in there. The overwhelming humidity of Jakarta was kept at bay by the icy air conditioning of the luxury MPV.

The Thai gentlemen were too polite to say anything about the long wait. I saw a look of confusion on the driver's face. I made eye contact with him several times. He shrugged and continue talking on his phone.

It was not hard to feel that inwardly the executives were wondering what the hold-up was about.

Finally, the driver ended his call, approached the car and walked around it. He opened the passenger side door and looked in. 'Gentlemen, apologies. There have been some unforeseen circumstances, and we cannot take the car today. You are going to have to get a taxi to the warehouse.'

'That's okay' Yut responded first. 'We would be happy to travel by any means.'

He was just being polite. It was quite clearly an inconvenience. I have learned along the way that you cannot get flustered in these situations. Like Yut, I took this in my stride and helped the driver unload the luggage from the car. To avoid the humidity, we walked into the hotel and awaited our alternative transport.

I made one last eye contact with the driver, and he gave me another blurred look and another shrug. Gosh!

The other executives were as well-mannered as Yut. Not a word was said about the disruption. Everyone remained perfectly calm and friendly. We made small talk while we waited.

'How do you normally deal with hot days like this?' one of them asked.

I replied, 'Well, ordinarily, we don't go outside.'
'Same same, we in Thailand also like that,' the other responded.

The group chuckled in chorus. The chuckles died out as an impeccably dressed businessman walked past us. He wore a suit, clearly an expensive one. He was younger than most executives, probably in his early thirties. To my surprise, he climbed into the rear of our MPV and signalled to the driver. He was the only passenger as it set off on its journey.

I commanded all my strength to hold on to my jaw so it wouldn't drop to the floor.

We looked at each other, but none of us passed comments on what we had just seen. I knew that at that moment, keeping silent was the best policy. There was no need to address the inference that the VIPs had been relegated to a taxi, while a single occupant was able to use the MPV. Any awkwardness created would only add more damage to our cause.

I kept calm, did my best to crack a few jokes, and naively hoped that our guests would forget the unforgettable.

Another 15 minutes went by, and we were now more than 30 minutes behind schedule. The taxi finally arrived. Well, it was two taxis. There were no taxis big enough to take all of us at once, so we had to split the delegation between two cars. We piled into the vehicles and were welcomed by the taxi drivers. The cars were not as luxurious as the MPV. There was air conditioning, but it was clearly an old unit, and the interior became stuffy fairly quickly. Besides, they were not spacious. We had to press up against one another, which was hardly the most comfortable of situations.

To make matters worse, the morning traffic was now in full flow. We were stuck in the stuffy, less than cosy cars for hours before we eventually reached the warehouse. In total, we were three hours late. The executives had the evening flight, so time was now of the essence.

Despite the adversity, the visit went well. As predicted, Eldon and I were able to answer all of their questions. They were impressed with the setup and technology of the warehouse. We managed to complete the visit in just a few hours, without missing out on any crucial details. Considering the morning's events, the tour was highly successful. In the late afternoon, they were picked up by more taxis and were taken to the airport.

As they were leaving, Yut shook my hand once more, 'Well done, that was perfect and highly impressive. Thank you for organising this successful trip. We'll be in touch with you shortly to work out further details.'

I bid farewell to Yut with a simple 'bye'. Well, I didn't know any more Thai phrases, so I figured 'bye' must be 'bye' in Thai too.

After they had departed, Eldon and I went for dinner. While we were eating, we discussed the morning's incident.

'Someone hijacked our MPV, and we had to leave our luxurious transporter and be bundled into the inferior taxis,' I told him.

Eldon turned stern and said 'Yeah, I know what happened there. He is from the integration team and is partially in charge of how our merger goes. The whole company is relying on him to get the merger done. Apparently, he was staying at the hotel and complained to the CEO that there was no car for him and that he was not going to take a taxi. He told the CEO that if he didn't get what he wanted, that she could lose her job during the merger.

There is only one CEO job, after all. So, he got what he wanted.'

Eldon played rugby: he was three times my size, and incredibly strong. If he were to dress in green, he could easily be mistaken for the incredible Hulk. After he finished his sentence, he added, 'if he had said that to me, I'd punch him on his nose and kick him on his butt and turn him into an instant eunuch!'

I believed him; Eldon would do that, literally, and he didn't really say 'butt'. It was something far more precious, and you know what I mean.

So, he held the CEO ransom to get what he wanted, with no consideration of the immediate future business. It was not just another business; it was a massive deal. He was a well-dressed man with a brain no bigger than the smallest peanut in the history of the planet Earth.

I did not know if the Thai executives would ever find out what happened there, but they were clearly unimpressed. We did not win the contract, and I felt that the lack of a smooth journey to the warehouse could have contributed to the unfavourable decision. If an organisation could not organise a simple car ride, how could they manage a large telco warehouse and the transportation services? Or perhaps the Thai executives saw a big crack in the merger exercise?

Losing the deal was a big let-down for everyone, except for that less-than-a-peanut-brain; he was in the integration team and he would not be held accountable for any revenue losses.

However, I was told that the integration team was completely dismantled a few months later. I did not know the reasons, and I didn't try to find out.

* * *

Power tends to corrupt and absolute power corrupts absolutely. When you assign power to people who are not ready to wield it, you are creating trouble for yourself and everyone else.

'You can fool some of the people all of the time, and all of the people some of the time, but you cannot fool all of the people all of the time.' -- Abraham Lincoln

16

THE NEGOTIATION

'You are cunning. You must have Klingon blood.'
-- *Lieutenant Worf*

Negotiation is something we do every day in various different ways. You negotiate with your kids when they want you to pick them up from school or from their friend's house in the evening or, more likely, when they want money.

'Dad! Can I have some money?'
'You've got money, I give you money every week.'
'I need some more money for school stuff.'
'What stuff?'
'School project.'
'How much?'
'How much is in your wallet?'
Etc, etc.

You negotiate the traffic when you drive into work every day, some motorists you let slip into your lane in front of you and some you refuse entry by running your car one centimetre from the car in front of you while staring directly ahead determinedly ignoring the existence of the car 2mm from your driver's window desperately trying to bully his way in front of you. I won't describe the conversation since it's generally not family-friendly. Note that I have deliberately avoided examples of negotiating with one's wife on account of the fact that such discussions are never really negotiations since husbands don't really have a choice and 'Yes dear' is normally the most advantageous response to any request: certainly it leads to the least pain.

Then there are the official work negotiations that you have to make with customers and suppliers. The danger here is that you need to do your homework well and know your costs well otherwise you could end up agreeing to a deal where you lose money.

In my experience it's best to come to a fair deal for both parties.

As a supplier of services, if I make a deal that is detrimental to me and I am losing money then I have to decide whether to continue or terminate. Continuing will mean potentially reducing my service level to cut costs or keeping the service level high and waiting until contract renewal (however many years later that may be) and increasing the rates then to try to recover the lost money – if your service level is very good then the customer won't want to change and may be agreeable to paying higher rates.

Similarly, if I charge rates that are too high then normally the customer will eventually realise this (all they have to do is get a quote from another service provider to compare), and the customer may be very upset since he/she is going to feel that he/she is being ripped off – a sure way to destroy a relationship.

There are always internal pressures on you when you are negotiating deals. Generally, finance people don't understand or really care about the customer since they never have to talk directly to them. Finance people tend to look at numbers on spreadsheets and demand more and more profit without really considering the long term partnership potential or even the soft benefits. Soft benefits may include taking on a customer with niche requirements that the operation has to learn how to do: such a soft benefit can help the service provider get experience and skill in providing specialised services that it can then offer similar services to new customers and hence grow the business. Finance does not normally see this as beneficial because it does not instantly translate to profit on the balance sheet.

This story tells of a work-related negotiation and stands out in all my experience as the most difficult one I've ever had to work through.

We had been providing logistics services to a principal for coming up to nine years. It was a specialised service due to the temperature control nature (it was very very cold) and we operated on a cost-plus model.

Cost-plus models are not the most popular in the logistics service provider world because the logistics provider is sharing every single expense with the principal and having to justify every bill every month, and then only taking a small management fee percentage for profit. It means that the principal knows how much money you are earning and has all the information they need to potentially take back the business from the provider and do the service themselves.

The principal could also simply replace the logistics provider with another one who charges a slightly lower management fee. The secret to maintaining such a principal is to build a relationship especially focused on transparency and trust.

In terms of transparency, the operation must admit any and all mistakes immediately, the principal must not find out later and suspect a cover up. In terms of trust, the logistics provider should support the principal with all special situations such as the principal wishes to expand or invest in the operations but has no budget (going through their own finance department is far too unpleasant) so the provider can put up the capital expenditure and charge back to the principal at a monthly fee as an operational expense.

We had a very good relationship with this principal over many years, we had also learnt a great deal from it and had used that learning to expand our own small cold chain operation for our own products. The principal was a very large famous company, so we were able to use their name as one of our customers in our marketing presentations to attract other principals.

There were a lot of 'soft' benefits to providing services to this customer that the finance team would not be able to put dollar signs against on the balance sheet thus it was always difficult to explain why we should continue to provide services when the profit was so small.

We were coming up to contract renewal again and the principal itself was going through some significant changes. Whereas in the past we had always dealt with the local country management, this time the renewal and RFP (Request for Proposal) process would be managed by the regional procurement team out of Singapore.

We had no relationship with the regional team so were instantly at a disadvantage. Our strategy then was to meet the regional team and start building a relationship with them. It started with a video conference.

The principal had a video conference meeting room in every country, very cutting-edge technology at the time, every meeting room in every country was designed exactly the same.

There was a large table with chairs for participants on one side and large LED TVs filling the wall on the other side. Cameras transmitted images of each participant to the LED TVs in the other country. The impression was that the other country was sat right in front of you across the table (although they were on TV screens). Even the tables in each country were identical so it suggested you were all seated in the same room.

The principal regional team was made up of Indian men. Our team sat excitedly in the video conference room waiting for everything to be connected. There were five of us including my boss.

The LED TVs suddenly sprang to life and we could see the regional procurement team members coming into the room; there were three of them, all Indian. Two were taking their seats. We could hear them chatting to each other and one had obviously been there a while since he was finishing his lunch. I remember he had only a banana left, and he began peeling it, almost erotically.

'Are we on?' asked the Indian with the banana; he was the principal procurement team boss as we would learn later.
'Hello?' he called out. 'Can you hear me?'

The first words uttered from our side came from my boss. 'Nice banana!' he said loudly.

Fortunately, the procurement head had a sense of humour and laughed at this: my boss had successfully broken the ice.

We all made our introductions and then the principal side made theirs. The procurement team head (having consumed his banana, less erotically than he had peeled it I might say) introduced his team, in particular the elderly Indian chap on his right whose name for the sake of this story we shall call Ramit.

'Ramit,' the procurement head said, 'will be leading the negotiation for the principal.'

Ramit introduced himself. He spoke very quickly with a strong Indian accent and all of my team in the room, including my boss, had no clue what he had just said.

The only word I could make out was 'I' which is the word he started his sentence with and even that I could have misinterpreted. Our whole team was shocked and we all just looked at each other's faces in panic as if to say: 'Did you understand anything he just said? Please say you understood!'

One of our team took the plunge after several seconds of silence.

'I'm sorry, could you repeat that please!' This was going to be a phrase used in extreme over the next six months.

Ramit repeated in exactly the same way.

It was marginally better. I was sure now that the first word he spoke was 'I', but the other words were still a mystery.

The conversation continued, fortunately mostly with the procurement head speaking who was clearly comprehensible.

Whenever Ramit spoke we were all clueless. We tried suggesting he speak slowly, and it helped a bit, we caught one or two more words. Sometimes it was enough to guess the meaning of what he was trying to say so we could provide some intelligent response. Mostly though, we were entirely in the dark as to what the hell he was talking about, and all this did was put pressure on every member of our team.

At one point we asked him to spell the word he was trying to say but we couldn't even understand what letters he was trying to articulate.

After the meeting we were all dumbstruck with shock. How were we going to negotiate with this guy when we couldn't understand a word he was saying?

Since my boss and I were English and we were able to understand more than anyone else on the team (but not much more), it was decided that my boss and I would lead the negotiation – much to the relief of the rest of the team.

The negotiation went on for six months. Ramit was a canny negotiator and he may have been using his strong accent to his advantage.

Sometimes he would say something and end with the sentence 'Do you agree?', with those three words being the only words we could understand.

The urge to say 'Yes' was almost overwhelming since we so badly wanted every discussion to end and we so wanted to understand what he was saying, so we would almost just say 'Yes' to mean 'Yes! Some words I understand!'.

Ramit also tended to call me and my boss separately, I believe in the hope of getting us to contradict each other in order to undermine our negotiating premise. My boss wisely decided early on that both he and I must be present for every conversation with Ramit, at the very least it would give us double the chance to understand what he was saying.

We tried to get Ramit to write down in an email a summary of his points after every telecon so that we could read what he was trying to communicate, but strangely, he refused to do so. Consequently, I would summarise each telecon in an email and send it out to all parties with the hope that if I had misunderstood anything, he would modify the email.

It didn't work. If I misunderstood anything, he would call me to clarify and that didn't help at all.

Ramit wanted to change the model from a cost-plus to an activity-based costing. We couldn't understand why he would want to do this since cost-plus was the most beneficial model a principal could have.

He would not be moved and insisted on us quoting for every activity, which we did. It then came down to negotiating every activity rate which led to a very painful few months of telecons with him every other day.

As mentioned, there were many unique cases where we had supported the principal over the last eight years such as capital expenditure purchases that we had made for assets in the principal's site and the principal was paying us back for that investment.

Ramit eventually had to concede that such payments would have to continue until the investment was fully paid for. We had a long list of exceptional rates and payments that Ramit, reluctantly, agreed to after many long incoherent conversations, and after we had the local principal team support us on it.

Finally, we were selected to continue providing the service for the new contract.

It was an activity-based costing contract instead of cost-plus so we no longer had to go through the P&L (Profit & Loss) and all expenditure every month with the local team. We just had to pull out the report from the principal's system on the number of total transactions performed during the month and multiply by the agreed rate for that transaction. Then add on all the exceptional payments that had been agreed to in the contract.

Ultimately, the total cost to the principal increased by 20%.

My finance manager was very happy. The local principal finance people were furious.

They naturally complained to the regional procurement team for negotiating such a terrible deal with us. My boss and I had a telecon with the procurement head (the one with the banana), who shouted angrily at us for twenty minutes.

We explained that we were always happy to retain the old cost-plus method but Ramit insisted on an Activity-Based costing method, so what could we do?

We proposed a solution to work with the local team to implement cost-savings projects to help reduce the costs to the principal, which we did quite effectively.

The last I heard, Ramit had been transferred from the Singapore office to Russia – seems they had sent him to the Gulag!

In a normal situation I would have loved to know what he had to say about that but in this case, I was glad not to.

* * *

If you can put yourself into the other side's shoes and understand their pain points, then you have a good chance of reaching a win-win conclusion to any negotiation. Our pain point was that we couldn't understand what he was talking about and he must have known this but made no attempt to relieve our pain. Ultimately, it resulted in a win-lose outcome where we were simply lucky to be on the winning side.

'You do not get what you want, you get what you negotiate.' -- Harvey Mackay

17

SUPERMAN

'KHHHHAAAAAAAAN!'
-- *Captain James T. Kirk*

'I have done it so many times, you just get one of your programmers here, and everything will be solved,' Mr Kho shouted into his phone.

I was there, in front of him, waiting patiently for him.

After about 10 minutes of heated conversation, he finally put down his phone. Perhaps I should not refer to it as a conversation, for that implies a two-way communication. Mr Kho had been yelling non-stop into the phone and repeating the same statement.

'Sorry to keep you waiting, I just had to pressure the vendor, kick them so they move,' he gave me a big but rather cold smile.

'It's okay,' I was polite, 'what seems to be the problem?'

'No problem, we need to change the system a bit, we just need one programmer from the vendor to sit with us, and everything will be okay,' he replied.

'Hasn't the system already gone live? I thought your operation is using it now?' I asked.

'Yes, that's why we find out something is not correct, and we had already made a lot of changes and just want to make a few more changes to the software,' he answered casually.

I was sent to the warehouse by Mr Kho's boss who contacted me through a referral. We met up for a drink in a restaurant on Temple Street Singapore, and he told me his warehouse had gone live with a WMS (Warehouse Management System), and since then he was facing many issues, so he wanted me to visit his warehouse and give him some feedback, and to ensure he would not face the same problems after he switched to our warehouse software.

Mr Kho was the General Manager, a Malaysian who had worked in Singapore for a few years. He said he had many years of experience and had managed many warehouses before joining the company. He also said that he had extensive experience with several WMS.

However, the statement he just made was frightening. He should not be making a lot of changes to the system after it had gone live.

'I want to tell you that I don't think there are any opportunities here for you, we don't really need your consultation. I have done a lot of WMS, it is not as simple as you thought, and it is hard for you to understand the operations. Our WMS is fine, just need a programmer to be here to change the programs.' Mr Kho said, continuing with his smile, and carried on insisting that everything was okay by his standards.

It seemed like his boss did not tell him all the details, and he didn't know the real reasons I was in the warehouse.

'Well, I hope to understand more, and just out of curiosity, how long have you gone live with the new system?' I asked.

'About four months,' he said while keeping his smile, but I could sense that there was a bit of impatience mixed with agitation, and I felt that he had just shot me with a look that was so cold, it was about to pierce through me.

'Your boss told me it was six months,' I confronted him.

'Oh Ya… about four to six months,' he replied unhappily. I was pretty sure that he would have pulled out a shotgun on me if he had one, but we were in Singapore, where it was a capital punishment to have a gun, so I felt safe.

Six months was a very long time for a WMS to stabilise, given that his warehouse was not a complex one.

'Your boss said that the system is having many issues, so he wanted me to understand those issues,' I said, trying to keep my voice in a monotone. I was expecting more resistance.

'You see, there are no issues. I have been doing this for many years, I have been through a lot of new system implementations in the warehouse. I am arranging the vendor to send me a programmer, and everything will be okay. My boss should give me some time to do it,' he tried to control the volume of his voice, but it was evident that he was getting very unhappy with my presence.

'Looks like the programmer is a Superman, he can fix all the problems,' I couldn't help but be a little sarcastic.

'Oh ya, he is a Superman, and we also call him Superman. He works so hard, and he has helped us solve all our problems,' Mr Kho responded, oblivious to the sarcasm.

'So how many changes have you made to the system?' I asked.
'I don't know, we don't really count them,' he answered with a shrug.

'Does Superman know?' I asked.
'No, Superman takes instructions from me. He focuses on fixing issues,' he answered.

'But you don't know how many changes are made to the system?' I asked.
'No, I know, but I didn't count them, it was not important as there are many other more important things to do,' he answered.

I froze, scanned the room for aliens, thinking for sure they must have consumed a big chunk of his brain.

'I understand that there was an issue in the picklist and it was fixed, but the same issue reappeared again this morning?' I asked.
'Yes, it's a very small issue. When Superman arrives, he can fix it in one second,' he answered.

'Right, didn't Superman fix it the last time?'
'Oh, ya, that's right. You see, he had fixed it last time, so he can fix it again, very fast, one second.'

In software, once you have fixed something, it should not recur.

'How many times did Superman fix this same issue?' I asked.
'A few times, that's why he has the experience to fix them, he can fix it very fast, like in one second,' he replied.

Aliens! Brain-eating aliens! They must be hiding somewhere in this warehouse. Couldn't he tell that the issue was not fixed?

'What about the inventory report? I understand that the inventory report is showing different inventory quantity and some even have a negative quantity?' I asked.

'Yes, it is a small issue. Superman also can fix it easily,' he answered.

'Like how easy? Can Superman also fix it in one second?' I asked with unveiled sarcasm.

'I think this one will take a bit longer, maybe two or three seconds,' he answered with a humourless face as if he had thought it through.

Tell me you don't believe there were no brain-eating aliens in this warehouse too!

'And the delivery order? I understand that the quantity displayed is inconsistent with the actual picked and shipped quantity.' I asked.

'Yes, another small issue, Superman can fix it easily,' he answered. It looked like it was going to be his standard answer.

'So how many issues are pending to be fixed by Superman?' I asked.

'Not a lot, just a bit here and there,' he answered.
'I see, but how many?' I insisted.

'It is hard to say,' he replied.
'How so?' I was confused.

'You see, sometimes the system is okay, but another time the system is not okay, that's why we need Superman to be here,' sticking to his standard reply.

'Do you have a list to track all these issues?' I asked.
'No, there are not a lot of issues as you can see, Superman will fix them when he is here,' he answered.

I was no longer annoyed.

Are the aliens secretly feeding on my brain too?

'What is your inventory accuracy now?' I asked, and it was a trick question.

'I would say 99%,' he answered without a blink.

'How do you know it is 99%?'
'Oh, I know, it is very accurate.'

'I mean, does the system tell you it is 99%?'
'Oh, the system is very good. It can tell me,' he dodged the question.

I politely requested him to show me in his WMS the inventory of a few randomly selected ground locations in his warehouse. I wrote down the product name and quantity displayed in the system for each of the locations displayed. He didn't show me. He asked one of his people to show me. It looked like he was not comfortable with navigating his WMS.

I walked with him in the warehouse to those locations. My eyeballs rolled furiously scanning every corner for signs of aliens.

Given all the things I knew so far, there was a very high chance that the physical quantity would not match the quantity stated in the system.

I was right that not only was the quantity wrong, but the products stored at all the randomly selected locations were also different from what was stated in the system. It was as if the warehouse operation was not using the system.

'How could the inventory accuracy be at 99% when all the inventory in a few randomly selected locations were all wrong?' I tried not to sound like I was intimidating him.

'Do you know how many locations we have in this warehouse? You have just looked at a few locations, and you concluded that the accuracy is not good. Only after a stocktake is done, then you can conclude,' he replied, paused and then mocked me, 'it is basic warehouse 101, don't you know?'

After a long morning, he finally said something that I felt had a bit of intelligence in it. The aliens were not greedy. They hadn't taken everything from him.

I laughed and said, 'You are right, and I agree, the stocktake will give you a definite answer, but the Law of Averages tells you the trend.' I stopped and didn't want to imply anything more. In so many of my warehouse visits over the years, this was a rare occasion that I felt unsafe, and that there was an invisible line which I should not cross. I did not push the topic further.

'Anyway, all the locations you saw just now were accurate.' He said. I was shocked, and I didn't know what he meant; 'Pardon me?'

'Something is wrong with the system. After Superman fix the issues, the inventory will be accurate,' he said.

Did I hear him correctly, that he just suggested that he would instruct Superman to manipulate the data so that it looked right? I made a mental note of that and didn't respond to that statement.

'Can Superman fly here?' I tried to crack a joke.
'No, no, he usually takes a taxi,' he didn't think it was funny.

'When will Superman be here?' I asked.
'That's why I just call them, he will be here soon,' he answered.

'I see. How soon?' I pushed a bit.
'Soon!' he replied with an icy cold voice that made me chill. I really should stop the meeting: I did not feel safe.

There were metaphorical bullets in the air, that at least I was sure. The company had bled badly as a result and they were as yet unable to stop the bleeding. It was rare but not too uncommon for people in charge of the warehouse to manifest muddy inventory visibility, especially in small and middle enterprises.

I knew I would not get any clear answers from him, and I knew something was wrong. Terribly wrong.

He didn't know what and how many changes were made to the system.

He didn't know how many more fixes were pending.

He didn't keep records of anything.

He couldn't differentiate between change requests and bugs.

He lacked the experience of warehouse operations. As such, he was not capable of testing the system before the system went live, hence he needed to keep making changes after the system went live.

He didn't have any target dates for anything, and he didn't know when his vendor would come, he didn't know when the issues could be fixed.

And he wanted to manipulate the data in the system!

I suspected the vendor had made so many changes to the system that the entire system had become so buggy and unstable, it was highly likely they were unable to fix it anymore. These cases usually happen to software houses that attempt to modify their software to cater for more requirements without domain expertise. It was likely that the software had been changed so much that it was already beyond repair.

I left the warehouse. There was no point in continuing the conversation. Well, I confessed that part of me was also afraid of the hidden brain-eating aliens. I regretted very much that I was not able to meet Superman in person to shake his hand.

I went back to the office to meet Kho's boss. He was on a call when I arrived. He signalled me to go into his room, and he put the phone on speaker. A voice came through.

'I am sorry, we have lost a lot of money on this project, we cannot continue anymore.'

'Your loss? What about mine?' the boss said.

'I am really sorry, we have tried to accommodate every request from Mr Kho, we have put in a lot of effort, and all our resources were in this project for more than 12 months, we cannot afford to continue with this project anymore,' the voice said.

'So, what are you proposing?' the boss asked.

'We need you to increase your budget so we can modify our program to cater to your unique requirements,' the voice said.

'What type of budget?' the boss asked.

The voice gave a number, and the boss answered with a raised volume, 'this number is bigger than the entire contract amount, which we have already paid in full!'

'Yes, but you have a lot of unique requirements,' the voice answered.

The boss looked at me as if asking me if I had any questions.

I should not have, but out of curiosity, I just asked, 'Will Superman be involved in this new project?'

It seemed the voice didn't notice it was a different person who just spoke, and he answered, 'Oh no, Superman just left our company, we will be putting a new and more experienced team to do this.'

He put down the phone and asked for my opinion, and I remember vividly that all I said was 'Well, even Superman died on this project, do you want to give it another shot?'

I then shared my findings with him.

It was later discovered that the vendor had developed some small programs for a few warehouse customers. Then they marketed their software programs as if they were full-blown WMS software products. They had done an outstanding job in marketing, and with the recommendation of Mr Kho, the boss bought the software at a high price.

However, the people who developed the software were not industrial experts and had limited warehouse experience, so the software did not cater for many basic warehouse operation requirements. There were no experienced consultants who had the domain knowledge to guide Mr Kho. He then became the perceived expert and went wild on making changes to the system. It was like the blind leading the blind, and eventually, the system became so unstable it was beyond repair. Hence the vendor wished to have a new budget to start over.

It was devastating for the boss, not only would he need to pay a lot more for a WMS, but he had also wasted a great deal of time and effort in the ordeal. His company's brand had suffered damage as he continued to receive complaints from customers with the wrong products and quantities shipped to them along with all the incorrect documents printed from the system. He also did not know his inventory losses because all the figures provided by his system could not be trusted. He had to set up two teams to reconcile all the figures, and nobody could give him a single version of the truth.

I recommended him to replace the system, and I was glad that he accepted our offer. I knew we could help him, and we did.

* * *

The software, the consultants, the operation team and the bosses are all critical success factors of supply chain software projects. Be aware that expensive software and services may not always be good, but good software and services are always more expensive.

'If you pay peanuts, you get monkeys.' -- James Goldsmith

Beware, sometimes even if you pay more than peanuts, all you get is better-paid monkeys. Best to know what you are buying and pay the right price for it.

18

WORKING WITH COMPUTERS

'Computers make excellent and efficient servants,
but I have no wish to serve under them.'

-- *Spock*

My career began after university in the space industry where my role was officially a Production Engineer but I worked in the Manufacturing Systems Department where mostly I was a computer programmer. I'd been writing programs since I'd turned 13 when I got my first computer, a ZX Spectrum, a state-of-the art computer with 16k of RAM (hard drives for home computers in the early 80s was unthought of especially since 99.9% of the population at the time thought a hard drive was London to Manchester in a mini).

The ZX Spectrum was the size of an iPad but thicker, no screen - it plugged into the TV, programs were loaded and saved on audio tape, so you also needed to connect a tape recorder. There was no operating system such as Windows, you had to learn ZX Spectrum BASIC programming language in order to get the computer to do anything.

Consequently, the first programming language I learnt was BASIC. When I went to university, I learnt FORTRAN and while in the manufacturing systems department I learnt C++. For non-computer programmers you probably have no clue what I am talking about, if indeed you are still awake.

These are all programming languages, each one getting

progressively harder – like learning a second language, you start with something easy like Spanish and work your way through ever harder ones until you get to that clicking language in Africa (communicating by clicking sounds really hard but it may just be like Morse code).

The technology in the late 80s and early 90s, even at a high-tech company making rockets and satellites, was so far behind that of today.

We had IBM personal computers that cost thousands of dollars to buy so only the richest could afford to buy them and generally the richest were not computer savvy in those days. Most of the richest business people certainly did not believe that computers would one day be in everyone's home (Bill Gates and Steve Jobs were still kids working out of their home garage at this time).

I sometimes hear managers in 2020 laughing at low-tech companies' inferiority because they still use Lotus Notes email instead of Outlook.

When I started my career, Lotus Notes was the leading spreadsheet software: Microsoft had not yet come up with Windows 3.1 and we didn't use a mouse. When Windows 3.1 came out to revolutionise how computers were operated, I had to learn to use the mouse which I hated, I thought it was a terrible idea. I could never get the arrow to move exactly where I wanted it, most frustrating. I felt it was much easier to type the commands.

Hard drives were very small in the early 90s (we had one of the latest IBM computers; it had a 40-megabyte hard drive which was huge – compared with today when hard drives are routinely able to store 25,000 times more!). Programs were stored on other formats such as 3.5-inch floppy disks which weren't floppy at all (they were encased in hard plastic) or 5.25-inch floppy disks that really were floppy, or paper tape or paper cards (basically paper with holes in it) which were as floppy as it gets!

The factory I worked in purchased a brand-new Numerical Control machine for drilling holes in precisely the right place and precisely the right size in materials i.e. a computer-controlled drill.

This new NC machine had a 3.5-inch floppy drive reader; however, all our programs were still on paper tape.

The factory was spread out over a 2 kilometre square chunk of land. The paper tape reader was at one end in the 'Design Building' and the new NC machine was at the other end in the old factory building.

One of my jobs was to walk over to the design building to get the paper tape program from the design room (a roll of paper with holes in it). I then had to find an IBM 3270, this was probably the oldest computer we had, it had two 5.25-inch floppy drives and no hard drive. One floppy drive was for the operating system (in modern computers the operating system is installed on the hard drive in the computer and automatically starts when you turn the computer on).

The other floppy drive was for your programs (in modern computers this would be the 'My Documents' folder). I had to connect the paper tape reading machine (rather like a celluloid film projector) to the IBM 3270 computer, slot in the floppy disk with the operating system and boot up.

I would then need to slot in an empty floppy disk in the other drive and run the paper tape machine. I could then copy the program from the paper tape to the 5.25-inch floppy.

I would then have to go to another building where we had the only computer that had both a 5.25-inch floppy drive reader and a 3.5-inch floppy drive reader on the same machine. I could then copy the program to a 3.5-inch floppy disk (that wasn't actually floppy at all).

Finally, I would walk all the way back to the factory building and, at the risk of sounding pornographic, slot in the non-floppy (i.e. stiff) 3.5-inch floppy disk into the brand-new NC machine, press 'go' on the machine and it would drill all the holes in the right place. A fantastic example of British efficiency and poor IT humour in one paragraph!

I had some disasters even in my time in Space Systems. The shop floor where they built the nose cones for the rockets (that would house the satellites that we also built) used a computer system connected to theodolites for measuring the accuracy of the build.

The computer would create a 3D model (in numbers, not graphically – remember this was the early 90s, the height of computer graphics was Space Invaders and Pacman). It was the function of the Quality Assurance (QA) department to measure the skeleton structure of the recently built nose cone. To do this, QA had to balance small ball-bearing marbles all over it in key positions.

Due to my keen interest in all things computerised, I learned the system and would often help the QA guy measure the structure, usually at a weekend when I could earn overtime.

A computer nerd in the early 90s was not nearly as sexy (or as well paid) as a millennial computer nerd, in fact it was the opposite of sexy: I had no social life whatsoever so would have worked the weekends for free just so as not to be bored.

Using four theodolites set up around the structure, we would initially get a position fix on each theodolite using the computer to calculate, via triangulation, the exact position of each theodolite device.

We would then focus each theodolite on each ball bearing. The light reflected by the ball bearing would always focus on a point exactly in the middle of the ball bearing. Knowing the diameter of the ball bearing you could measure the position of that point relevant to the structure. Measuring from at least two other theodolites you could use triangulation (i.e. trigonometry – yes, I was one of the very few kids from school who got to actually use some of the stuff we learned), to work out the exact position of the point.

Putting these two things together we could know the exact position of a key point on the structure. Measuring ball-bearing locations at various key points, we could then build a picture of the object we were measuring (albeit mathematically). We then worked out how closely the actual structure matched with the design and, if it were within a specific tolerance, it could be signed off and approved.

One day the computer stopped working, it kept coming up with an error. We rebooted and still the same error message appeared.

We didn't know what the error was because it popped up on the monitor in German and this was before the internet so we couldn't just pull out our mobile phones and translate it.

The QA department had no idea what to do so they just looked at me. First, I opened up the code to see if there was any obvious flaw in it; the error appeared to show the line number in the code from which the error was coming from.

The first thing I noticed was that all the code was in German.

This was not BASIC, FORTRAN or C++, this was way beyond the very limited experience of a 21-year-old Production Manager Trainee.

'Hmmm,' I muttered trying to act knowledgeably. 'This is a Wang computer,' I explained (actually I read if off the front of the computer).

'It's German. Everything is in German. Anyone speak German?' Stupid question, this was England in the early 90s, we all spoke English although none of us probably knew how we knew English. We just spoke it.

All we knew was that different languages were sometimes spoken outside of England.

'What are you going to do?' asked Fred, the sarcastic shop-floor worker who'd worked there forever.

'I don't know,' said the QA supervisor. 'David, what should we do?'

I had no idea what to do either. The entire production floor was at a standstill because they couldn't move on with the build until QA had signed off on the accuracy of the skeleton structure. I took a dive. It wasn't really my decision to make what with being a trainee and not even working in the QA department, but no-one else had any other ideas.

'I suggest we wipe the drive and re-install the software from the original disks,' I said.

This idea was greeted with complete silence due to the fact that no-one had understood a single word I had just spoken (even though I had spoken it in English).

However, after a few seconds they all agreed it was a good idea as long as I understood I would be responsible for it.

The QA supervisor went back to the QA office and dug around in some dusty shelves and eventually found the original disks; I don't believe they had been touched in years.

With great misgivings I wiped the drive and reinstalled the program.

After a highly stressful three-hour installation, the computer beeped it was done. With great trepidation and crossing of all fingers and toes for luck, I ran the program.

The normal start screen flashed up.

Everyone cheered which was startling. I hadn't realised the entire production workforce was peering at the screen from behind where I was sitting on the production floor.

I selected the theodolite program; the computer hummed a bit and then threw out another error.

A different error.

The production workers chuckled and muttered that they knew all along my idea wouldn't work.

'Nice one,' said Fred. 'You've just destroyed the company,' he laughed and then sauntered off for a cup of tea.

I opened the code to check the lines where the error had occurred. It was still all in German and totally unintelligible to me.

In the end I had to call the German software company. They dug out their old documents from years ago, which took them a whole day to find.

Within these documents they had documented an error in the version of the program that we were using. It required a small code modification on line 88,512 or something, nothing more than adding a comma in the right place.

After completing this modification and saving the program I ran it again. To my enormous relief the program worked! It had taken two days to fix and the entire production had been brought to a complete standstill.

Fred just laughed. 'Tea break's over,' he shouted.

* * *

So many lessons learnt from this story, where to begin?

1. Everything looks better after a tea-break.
2. Computer bug fixing is not a spectator sport, best to do it in private.
3. If you stick your neck out remember it might get chopped off.
4. If you make changes to a program, write it down somewhere and don't forget it. This is probably the most important lesson.

'The computer was born to solve problems that did not exist before.' -- Bill Gates

19

REAL ANTIQUE

'Change is the essential process of all existence.'
-- Spock

I was once a speaker in an event to share my experiences with a small audience, mostly small and middle enterprise owners, on 'why and when businesses need to invest in a Warehouse Management System'.

Many business owners did not know how to interpret the signals flashing at them in their business, especially those coming from the warehouse and supply chain. They ignored the warning signals and allowed issues to snowball until it turned into a gigantic bullet which they were no longer able to dodge and then in a blink of an eye, they became irrelevant in the market.

So, I shared some of the vital signals they should pay attention to which will increase the chances of dodging those bullets zooming towards them. In some cases, they may not be able to dodge the bullet and might have to bite the bullet instead to make it disappear.

Jack approached me after the event and invited me to his office for a discussion. He was an IT manager, and his boss could not attend the event, so he was sent to it instead. He told me he was using the WMS I represented, and thought our team might be able to help him upgrade his WMS.

I told him I would be delighted to discuss further with him, but I was under a heavy travelling schedule, so the only date available for me was a few weeks later. I asked if the upgrade was an urgent matter, and he told me it was not urgent, and he could wait. I offered him the chance to have my team discuss it with him first, but he preferred to have me there to talk to his boss. So, we fixed the date to be six weeks later.

I called my software principal to seek more information on the prospect. They told me the name of the company was not listed in their user database, so as far as they were concerned, Jack's company was not a user of their software.

I thought perhaps Jack used another company, either a holding company or a subsidiary, to purchase the software licence, hence their name not appearing in the user database. Or maybe it was a different software, and Jack remembered wrongly.

Two weeks later, Jack called me on a Sunday morning. He requested the meeting to be moved forward, the issues he was facing had elevated to critical status. Back then, a remote video conference call was not popular, and he insisted on having a face-to-face meeting to discuss the matter.

I told him I was overseas, and I would have to adjust multiple meetings to accommodate his meeting. He was obviously under tremendous stress, so I told him I would make some phone calls the next day and would get back to him.

On Monday afternoon, he called me again. He told me that his issues were settled, and we could stick to the original plan. I had to be stoic. I had just used the morning adjusting the meetings so I could accommodate his request, and I had to call everyone to readjust the meetings again.

A week later, he called me again to request postponing the meeting for another three weeks.

So, our schedule was back to square one. After three weeks, I was to meet him six weeks later. I thought his issues were all resolved and there was no longer any urgency.

A week before the meeting, he called me again, requesting to have a meeting immediately. I told him I was overseas, so an immediate face-to-face meeting was not possible.

This time, I didn't offer to adjust my other meetings to accommodate his. He requested that I send him a proposal for a WMS software upgrade immediately. I told him I could not do that without understanding more, or at the very least, which version he was using.

He then told me the software version number. A number that sounded antique.
'When did you install the software?' I asked.
'About 20 years ago,' he blurted.

'Are you on maintenance?' I asked.
'No,' he replied.

'When did you last pay the maintenance?' I asked.
'About 18 years ago,' he replied.

Software, like cars, requires maintenance. But unlike cars, it does not need to be sent to the workshop periodically to replace parts. The software maintenance is there to provide peace of mind protection for the customers for software problems such as bugs and also guarantee an upgrade path. There are other benefits and pitfalls, which perhaps I will share in another story. For now, just keep in mind that without software maintenance, if you are having any software issues, your software provider is not obliged to assist, and if they do, it will likely cost you a lot.

'So, in the last 18 years, who maintained the software?' I asked.
'We do it ourselves, self-maintain,' he replied.

I asked incredulously 'How many people do you have?'
'Just me, and one more junior person assisting me,' he stammered.

I silently shuddered after hearing that. I had never seen any good outcome from any company in a similar situation.

'What seems to be the problem?' I asked.

'We need to upgrade the software,' he said.

'Why do you want to upgrade the software?' I asked.

'Ohh ... because the software is very old now, we want the latest version,' he replied.

That was not a valid reason, so I had to drill further, 'why do you need the latest version?'

'Because we want to install the software on a new server. I need a proposal from you immediately, please...' he almost sounded imploring, which gave me an ominous feeling.

I felt that he was not comfortable letting me know the entire truth. I wasn't sure what he was afraid of, but I was travelling, and under a very tight back-to-back meeting schedule, so I did not have too much time on the phone with him.

I told him I was not able to propose anything because I did not know what the problems were. He insisted I provide a rough cost to him, so he could talk to his boss to get additional budget for the upgrade. He asked me to provide at least the software licence price.

I told him I could not do that. Until I could be sure that our software fitted his needs, I did not want to propose anything.

I put down the phone and went on to attend all my meetings. At the back of my mind, I knew something terrible must have happened.

I visited Jack seven days later. When I saw him, his eyes were red, and there was visible darkness surrounding his eyes from his eyebrows to his cheekbones. With the effect of his thick, round, black-framed glasses, it was as if he had turned himself into a panda.

'Jack, what happened to you? Are you okay?' I was concerned.

'No, I haven't slept yet,' he said.

You did not need any intelligence to know that something had gone wrong.

I sat down with him in a small meeting room, and I asked if he wanted to postpone the meeting to attend to more urgent matters.

'No, I need your help,' he said, and he told me what happened.

Jack was in his mid-forties. He wore a dark blue t-shirt, torn jeans and torn sports shoes. He had been with his company for 20 years: it was his first full-time job. He had been taking care of the WMS since the day the system went live. He was a very technical person and he was a fast learner. By the end of the second year, his boss asked him if he could maintain the WMS without the software vendor.

He performed an act of blind heroism and replied he could, and then his company faithfully terminated the maintenance contract with the software vendor.

The company owned a big warehouse and provided warehouse and logistics operation services for its customers. It was a third-party logistics company. Twenty years ago, the company was very big.

The WMS software was indeed an old version of the WMS I represented. In 20 years, my software principal had been acquired by another bigger software company, and then the bigger software company was later acquired by another even bigger software company. So, the ownership had changed hands twice and, because Jack was no longer on maintenance and after so many years, his record was no longer in the user database.

Jack was a technical person, and he was a programmer. Over the years, he had also done some small programs to complement the WMS. For example, he wrote a small program to read data from the WMS database and send SMSes to his boss's mobile phone.

I guessed that his boss must have been thrilled because he did not need to pay any maintenance fees. Jack could take care of everything.

And Jack did it well, he stayed in the company and maintained the system for 18 years.

So, what could go wrong?

As I was about to ask the question, an elderly lady opened the door without knocking, and said in an icy tone to Jack, 'system went down again, please get it sorted out. Now!'

Without having any eye contact with me, and without waiting for a reply from Jack, she just closed the door and walked away. It was abrupt.

Jack smiled, a bitter one, and said, 'give me a minute.'

He picked up his phone and called someone, and said, 'Let's do the same thing, reboot everything and if it doesn't work, let's scan the hard disk for all the bad sectors again.'

It was a quick call. When I asked him if I should excuse myself so he could get back to the urgent matters, he responded: 'Nothing much I can do now, just hope that the environment could last a bit longer, and I need your help.'

It turned out that the old version of WMS was running on an old version of Microsoft SQL Database Server, and using an old version of Microsoft Server operating system and an old version of whatever software had been installed on the server. All the software, including the WMS had reached End-Of-Life (EOL), meaning the respective software vendors no longer supported them.

Well, they were all EOL a long time ago. Jack and his company still used them for many years after EOL.

The problem? All the old server hardware was about to breakdown, and all the new hardware was not supported by the EOL software.

Big problem! They had unintentionally planted a time bomb for themselves, and nobody knew when it would go off.

After running non-stop for 20 years, the motherboard on the servers could just go kaput any time. The network card, graphic card and hard disk were all showing signs of being worn out. Even if Jack wanted to buy and was willing to pay, none of the hardware was any longer available in the market.

'It is a serious matter, why did you want to postpone the earlier meeting?' I asked.

'I found some old server parts at that time, so the boss thought that he could continue to use the servers for another few more years, and it would then be a waste of money to upgrade the server,' Jack replied.

I squinted. How incredulous!

Jack continued, 'Those old server parts were all second hand quality, and they are not any newer than our old server. We replaced one of the controller cards, and it went kaput in just two weeks.'

Why only make efforts at the very last minute? It was like digging a well only when thirsty.

'Who was the lady just now?'

'She was the boss's wife.'

Okay, that explained her behaviour. It was clear that she did not appreciate Jack's effort and loyalty.

Jack's phone rang, and after answering the call, he exhaled and said, 'the server is up and running again.'

He then called his boss, and after talking to him, he said to me, 'I am sorry, my boss needs to rush out for another meeting, we need to reschedule another time with him. In the meantime, I would appreciate your help in giving me a rough estimate for the project.'

We did not get very far with the cost estimation. We got stuck at item number one, which was the software licence. I gave him an estimate of the licence cost, and he wanted an almost 90% discount.

'You see, our IT budget was very low for the past 18 years, my boss would not approve the budget,' he explained, 'Can you call your principal, help us to talk to them, let them know that we are their loyal customer and have been using their software for the last 20 years. Maybe we can just pay for the maintenance, and they can give us a version to upgrade.'

To reinstate the software maintenance, he would need to pay for a reinstatement fee plus all the maintenance fees from the day it was terminated until the day it was reinstated. In his case, he would need to pay for 18 years of maintenance fees plus the reinstatement fee. It would be much cheaper for him to buy new licences.

I explained that to him, but he didn't understand the concept, he wanted to pay only one year's worth of maintenance fees, and he wanted the amount to be the same as what he had paid for 18 years ago, and then he wanted the latest WMS software to be installed immediately. To him, this meant upgrade.

The offer was just not realistic, and I told him I could not do it. He wanted me to call the software principal, and I told him I would, but it might take more time.

To my astonishment, he blurted, 'It's okay. We can wait.'

I left, and on my way back, I called my software principal to update them on my encounter and requested a special discount.

A week later, I got an offer from my software principal. They had received approval for a discount, something I felt was generous, but not as steep as Jack was expecting.

I called Jack and his sister answered the call. I could barely hear her as she was sobbing aloud. I was shocked to find out that Jack had had a serious accident.

He survived but would be hospitalised for a long time.

I called his boss and told him about the special offer. He was expecting the discount that Jack had asked for, which I told him was impractical. He was not happy and became resentful. He never called me again.

I was told that the company got into a lot of trouble a few weeks later. I suspected that their hardware had finally thrown in the towel after serving them for 20 years.

With the only person capable of resurrecting their old software and old hardware in hospital, their warehouse was not able to function properly. They were not able to calm all the screaming customers, and they lost almost all of them in no time.

They had a chance to dodge the bullet, but they didn't.

* * *

If your business relies on the performance of your software then you should partner with your software vendors, make sure they have your back.

'Penny wise and pound foolish.' -- *Robert Burton*

20

WORKING WITH PEOPLE

'If you prick me, do I not leak?'

-- Data

Just as computers can sometimes be difficult to understand and work with, people can be equally difficult or even more so. Computers are really stupid. You have to program them, feed them the right information for them to be useful and then interpret the information coming from them in the right way.

I, as a typical example of a person, can also be stupid.

I don't mean that I am stupid, only that on occasion I can be. In the same way as computers, I can say stupid things on account of not having the right information or on account of thinking about the information in a different (though not necessarily wrong) way, or on account of being unable to clearly articulate the results of my thinking, leading to my listeners misinterpreting them.

A logistics example of this is when we built a cost model on a warehouse that stored products from many different principals. We wanted to know how much it really cost to service each principal when the warehouse, staff and transport costs were all shared.

In reality, every day would have a different cost to each principal. If on Monday, principal A had most of the orders then most of the staff time and the transport would be used to pick and deliver principal A's orders.

However, if on Tuesday, principal A had very few orders, but principal B had many orders, then resources (hence cost) would be spent on servicing principal B. It was important to take averages over a long period of time, such as one full year, to estimate the amount of resources and hence dollars spent servicing each principal on average.

The finance department of the company subtracted the average cost per principal from the principal income and worked out which principals were the least profitable. They then, moronically, terminated any principals that made a loss based on this math.

The result was that those principals who were terminated no longer stored their products in our warehouse, so we were carrying less stock and shipping fewer orders, however, the warehouse rental we had to pay was the same and the staff level was the same, so we ended up paying the same for overall less income.

When we recalculated the cost model, the finance team was aghast because the same cost had now been spread over fewer principals and the cost to service each principal on average was higher than before. Finance then planned to terminate more loss-making principals. The company was very intelligent to come up with a super model for estimating the cost to serve, but really stupid on how they interpreted the results. As the saying goes, 'an intelligent person knows that a tomato is a fruit, but a wise person knows not to use a tomato in a fruit salad'.

Even the smartest people can be stupid especially if they believe their own hype.

I once worked with a Chief Financial Officer who was an elderly lady who diligently worked her way to the top of an international company and was clearly highly intelligent, not least because she had proven it by reaching the giddy heights of CFO. I remember her well because she tended to have severe mood swings. She would swing from annoyed to really annoyed to downright abusive and back again.

During a very large system implementation project, she was clearly a little out of her depth with the IT terminology, yet, as CFO, she clearly also felt that she knew more about anything than anyone else. Ours was a logistics distribution business and her favourite pastime was to heckle me on my transport costs every time we met and complain that I spent too much money on transport for delivery.

The terminology employed by the consultants for the system implementation included the word 'transport' to mean 'copying signed off tested programs from the test server to the production server'. Such transports would only take place on a Friday night so that if there was any issue with the new program then we could fix it over the weekend and reduce the risk to the service when the business started operations again on the Monday.

One day, the IT project manager sent an email to management and everyone on the project to inform us that on the coming Friday there would be server maintenance and no transports would take place. Immediately the CFO responded with an email to me and including in cc everyone in the company, demanding that I put in place extra trucks to ensure deliveries on time due to the upcoming IT transport stoppage.

The smartest people can sometimes look like idiots when they are put into an environment that they are totally unfamiliar with or uncomfortable with. It can elicit the same reaction as that of a rabbit crossing the road at night when a car is approaching.

The rabbit is a very fast runner yet is unfamiliar with the sound of the car and the brightness of the headlights and instead of easily running to safety gets splattered all over the road.

The classic 'rabbit in the headlights' moment for management often takes place at staff parties since these are a time for the top management of a company to make total assholes of themselves. I have a very poor voice for singing and little body coordination for dancing, couple that with body areas that are larger and rounder than they probably should be, and the image of Taylor Swift is not what comes to mind.

Yet, every year, as a manager in my company I was compelled to get on stage to dance and sing a song in front of the staff. My company was not small and staff parties had up to 5,000 people or more attending them. Singing karaoke badly in front of a few friends could almost be considered fun if enough alcohol is involved. Singing with a live band badly while sober in front of 5,000 people is another level of humiliation altogether.

I remember one of the first staff parties I had to put together when the company was still very small and there was only around 800 people, I didn't even ask the management team to sing a song, only to dress up in fancy clothes, but they failed to have even the imagination to do that.

Consequently, my staff party team arranged the fancy clothes for them. One of the managers was almost sick with nerves before going on stage. He was dressed rather lamely with two other managers as basketball players and so was just in shorts and a basketball shirt. In front of the cheering crowd he got stage fright and froze. All he had to do was catch the basketball from his colleague; instead the ball hit him in the head and knocked him off the stage.

Fancy dress very soon became simply not enough for the larger rowdier crowds of staff members who wanted to see their management look like fools. Karaoke was the tool of preference.

I have had some experience with karaoke from doing a traumatic version of Livin' on a Prayer by Bon Jovi in an early karaoke bar in the UK in the 80s all the way to singing Staying Alive by the Bee Gees in a breaking falsetto in a dark Myitkyina bar in a remote northern province of Myanmar 30 years later. A previous staff party had me singing Britney Spears 'Baby one more time' – selected maliciously by my HR department.

However, the one singing event that is likely to lead to the most psychiatric sessions will always be singing 'Go West' by the Village People. My boss and I were to perform a duet of this song. My boss who had had all introvert genes removed since birth insisted that we do a synchronised dance routine. Singing badly was not enough, we also had to throw our bodies around in a wildly hilarious fashion in synch.

We choreographed and practised a dance routine for weeks.

On the big day of the show we decided to indulge in some Dutch courage prior to the gig leading us to be late arriving (and a little tipsy). Picture the scene: two large sweaty white guys running through Bangkok in 35°C heat, one wearing a soldier's uniform and the other dressed like Admiral Nelson.

We got to the venue just in time. No time to think or worry about the gig, we went straight on. Live band, lights, cameras, live video footage broadcast around the huge venue on giant screens so those at the back of the enormous hall could get to see us in all our humiliating detail.

We sang the song and danced the routine all perfectly according to plan. With the one small exception.

We were singing and dancing 'Go West' while the band was playing 'YMCA'.

It can sometimes be important to ensure that all your staff are aligned in presenting a certain impression to customers, especially when trying to win a new principal business, and you want your principal to believe that both your companies run on common values since this can help to quickly build trust.

There was the time that my Warehouse Manager, an Australian chap, heavy built and a keen weightlifter, was showing the CEO from a potential principal around our warehouse.

The CEO was a New Zealander, also a tall burly chap. Plenty of testosterone was flowing and lots of manly jokes were cracked as they wandered the warehouse floor. They visited the security room and admin offices and eventually, late in the evening, arrived at the customer service offices.

Being late, the customer service team had already gone home so it was quiet. As they wandered around the office the visiting CEO stopped at one cubicle and his jaw dropped.

The walls of the cubicle were covered in posters of naked, oiled up, muscular men.

I am sure that had the posters been of naked women then it would have been perfectly acceptable, but the images of naked men took the wind out of the visiting CEO's lungs.

My burly boss turned around to see what was holding up his friend and on seeing the pictures he nearly fainted.

The new millennium has brought so many changes. I grew up working with my dad who was a mechanic and spent a large amount of time in his garage which was littered with calendars of semi-naked female models. This was normal for most 70s and 80s workshops in the UK, all the tool makers and part makers used to give away thousands of naughty calendars every year.

Now, we have naked and semi naked men posters.

Interestingly, it's still the men putting them up on the walls of their workplace. Just not the same kind of men!

Our customer service department was staffed by mostly women who tended to have a kindly voice and nicer way of dealing with angry customers calling in. However, we also had a couple of gay chaps who were even better at defusing tension on a phone call than the girls.

Naturally, the warehouse manager had a few terse words with the customer service staff the following day and the posters suddenly disappeared.

I think the visiting CEO was helped over this traumatic experience with a sweaty work out in the gym with the warehouse manager and a few stiff drinks afterwards, as we still won the account.

* * *

If a manager surrounds himself with like-minded people, then he/she will always get like-minded ideas rather than new inspiration. Embracing diversity is like trying new cuisine, it may not always be as appealing to you as it is to others.

I believe that a manager should not be expected to know everything which would be pretty arrogant but should have the judgement and temperament to make sound decisions and the humility to fix those decisions that were maybe not so sound. Oh, and a good singing voice is very much a 'nice to have'.

'Management is efficiency in climbing the ladder of success; leadership determines whether the ladder is leaning against the right wall.' -- Stephen Covey

GLOSSARY

2D Barcode – 1D barcode is the name given for a normal flat barcode, for example, printed on a label attached to virtually every product in a supermarket. 2D barcode looks like squares that have many dots. 3D Barcode has another element, which is the height of each line, it is the name given to a QR barcode that can be scanned using your phone and a QR reader app and is normally engraved onto the product.

Access Points – Receptors in the warehouse for picking up and transmitting radio frequency signals.

Business Case – This is not a special bag for business documents. When a department in a company wants to buy something expensive, normally the finance department demands to know why, so the department has to explain why they want to buy it and why it would be good for the company. The report explaining this is called a business case. Usually it is delivered to the finance department in a special bag for business documents.

CAPEX – Capital Expenditure. If a company buys something expensive such as a building, a truck or a hundred computers, the cost is so high that it could wipe out the profit of the company for the entire year or even longer. This does not help the company's share price and may deter people from investing in the company. It's also not fair to the company because the asset they have bought is still worth a lot of money. Consequently, the law allows accounting rules to depreciate the value of the asset purchased over a number of years. If you buy a brand-new computer for US$1000 then on day one the computer is still worth US$1000. However, every year the computer gets older its value becomes less. After about five years the resale value of the computer is virtually zero. Accounting rules will depreciate the computer over five years so, after one year the computer is still worth US$800, after two years it is still worth US$600, etc.

CCTV – Closed Circuit Television. Such cameras are nowadays routinely placed all over the warehouse to cover every conceivable angle and the resulting video is maintained for months in case investigation is required. More recently the cameras are high-definition so that significant detail can be seen and zoomed in on to support such features as facial recognition.

Certificate of Analysis – also usually associated with pharmaceuticals, a document describing the products that need to be delivered together with every order.

Container (40-footer) – Standard containers were invented by Malcom Maclean in 1956 and essentially revolutionised transport and trade. Instead of trying to load (and unload) all different sizes of products and container boxes to a ship or a truck, the containers were suddenly all the same size and shape. Standardised equipment was built to load and unload them quickly from ships as well as standardised trailers that could drive them to their destinations directly from the port. There are two sizes of container, one is 40-feet long (40-footer) and the other is 20-feet long (20-footer).

Cycle Count – the counting of stock in specific areas of the warehouse on a regular basis or cycle. Nothing to do with counting bicycles.

Delivery lead time – the time needed to deliver the product to a customer from receiving the customer's order.

Demand Planning and Forecasting System – normally uses historical data to estimate how much of a certain product is likely to be sold in the near future such as over the next three months. By offsetting the expected sales with the actual stock on hand the system can advise the factory how much more product should be manufactured in order to meet customer demand.

Distribution Centre (DC) – a fancy name for a warehouse.

Drive In – A type of racking. Selective racking and VNA racking allow for one pallet to be put into or taken out from a location at one time. Drive in racking allows for many pallets to be crammed into one location and requires the forklift to (carefully!) drive into the racking to put away or pick out a pallet at the back.

Enterprise Resource Planning (ERP) – the name of the main sales and finance system for handling sales orders and accounting.

GPS – Global Positioning System, used in logistics mostly for tracking delivery trucks or delivery people so that the customer can be informed in real time on where their order is and if it is nearby.

First Expiry First Out (FEFO) – system for allocating stock to orders. The products that are due to expire first should be picked and delivered first.

ISO – International Organisation for Standardisation which would logically make the acronym IOS; unfortunately this one has been taken so instead it can be remembered as the International Standards Organisation.

IT – Information Technology.

Item master – also known as the product master or material master. It is the list of all the different products sold by the company and / or stored in the warehouse.

Key Performance Indicators (KPIs) – a measure of how well the logistics' provider delivers the products, such as how many orders they delivered on time during the month or how many mistakes they made.

Material Handling Equipment (MHE) – Anything used to move the products around the warehouse. It could be a forklift truck or a hand pallet jack or even a trolley.

Mezzanine – a temporary structure often built inside a warehouse to provide additional levels of floor space.

Pallet (PL) – a base plate on which products are stacked and that can be moved around easily with equipment such as a forklift and safely placed in racking for storage. It is often made from wood or plastic, comes in a variety of sizes but mostly there are two standard sizes: in Europe the size is 1 x 0.8m, in the US the size is 1 x 1.2m.

Picking List – For each order, the WMS will create a picking list for each area of the warehouse that products need to be picked from. For instance, for an order for products from the freezer room and from the normal ambient room, the WMS will create the picking list on two pages since different people will take each page and go to the required rooms to pick the product.

Poison form – usually associated with pharmaceuticals. It is a legal requirement, when delivering prescription drugs, for a pharmacist at the warehouse to pick and check the drugs are correct for the order, and for a doctor at the hospital or clinic to confirm the drugs are correct and sign for them.

Radio Frequency (RF) – RF devices in a warehouse are like smartphones with built-in barcode scanners that connect to the main warehouse computer via radio frequency. For instance, when you put a product away in the warehouse you need to note down the location code of where you put it and then go to the computer and confirm the code in the database. With an RF device you can simply scan the location barcode wherever you are in the warehouse and immediately update the database.

Reach Truck – a forklift that can reach up very high but the driver remains in the cab at floor level.

Return on Investment (ROI) – if a company buys a new machine then it is expected that the machine will generate new profits for the company. For instance, if the machine can make 1 million bottles of fruit juice a year and each bottle sold generates US$1 of profit then the machine can generate a profit for the company of US$ 1 million a year. If it costs US$3 million to buy the machine, it will take three years of profits to pay for the machine. The ROI is therefore three years.

RFID – Radio Frequency Identification, essentially a barcode that can be read using radio frequency scanners instead of a barcode scanner meaning it can be read more easily than having to line up the scanner onto a physical barcode. There are normally two kinds of RFID, active and passive. Passive RFID tags require a reader nearby to scan to pick up the RFID signal. Active RFID tags issue a signal that can be picked up from further away. Active RFID tags are normally more expensive and require battery power, and the battery will eventually die; passive tags should logically last forever.

RFP/RFQ – Request For Proposal / Request For Quote. Any time a company wishes to hire the services of a third-party logistics company they will prepare a document explaining their requirements and what prices they want to quote for in an RFP or RFQ document.

Route Planning System – Often part of a TMS, it automatically arranges orders into specific routes for grouping in one truck for delivery.

Scope Creep – the biggest danger to all IT projects. Before implementing an IT system, it is advised to agree with all parties on what they want the IT system to do. The system can then be designed to do what everyone wants it to do. Sometimes people forget to include some functionality in the original design and ask that the new IT system performs this additional function. The system was not initially designed for this new function and adding it may cause deficiencies in the other functions. Adding on new functions later can lead to low performance or failure of the most important functions.

Server – the main computer and it may also be where the central database is located.

Sprinkler – system of water pipes throughout the warehouse connected to special valves that will open when there is a fire and spray the water over the fire area.

Stock Keeping Unit (SKU) – a specific product and size, for example, a 33ml can of beer is one SKU, a 650ml can of the same beer is another SKU and a bottle of the identical beer is another SKU. Doesn't have to be beer, can be any product but logistics people tend to think about beer a lot.

Third Party Logistics (3PL) – an outsourced service (third party) hired to provide logistics services. such companies normally comprise trucks, warehouses and very large men.

Transportation Management System (TMS) – A system for managing deliveries and fleets of trucks.

Turret Truck – a forklift that can reach up very high and will take the driver up together with the forks.

User-defined fields – an IT term. A field is a data item often keyed in by the users such as a name, a number or a date. Many systems have pre-defined fields so the format is pre-set to be text, a number or a date. User-defined fields allow the user to create their own specialised data fields in the system.

Very Narrow Aisle (VNA) – Warehouses tend to install shelves for storing pallets of product on, called 'Racking'. There are many different types of racking, but the most common is called 'Selective Racking' and is simply racks with a gap between them (aisle) of 2-4 metres to allow people and forklifts easy access. VNA as the name suggests has a much narrower aisle around 1-1.5m and needs guide rails for the special forklifts to ensure they don't accidentally crash into the racking.

Warehouse Management System (WMS) – a software and database of all the products in the warehouse and where they are kept, in the old days used to be known as 'storeman's head'. Advanced WMS has the capability to govern the operation flow and streamline processes to make the warehouse operation more efficient.

WIFI – stands for Wireless Fidelity and means pretty much the same as RF. It facilitates the transfer of information between computers and devices using radio frequency.

Yard Management System – Automatically assigns a queue number and a dock number to a truck at the warehouse that is waiting to either unload new products inbound or pick up orders for outbound delivery. It also keeps track of all the products stored at the yard, for example containers.

ABOUT THE AUTHORS

Aw Yang Uei graduated from the University of Waterloo, Canada with a Bachelor of Mathematics (Honours) degree in Computer Science. He started his own business, focusing on supply chain and logistics software in the year 2000. He has represented many top international software brands such as Manhattan Associates, Infor and Blue Yonder (formally known as JDA and Red Prairie). He started his business with 10 dollars and today he has offices in Singapore, Malaysia, Thailand, Hong Kong, Shanghai and Taiwan.

David Mouland graduated from City University London with a BSc (Hons) degree in Aeronautical Engineering and was a manufacturing system engineer in the space industry before becoming a traveller and English teacher who then inexplicably turned into a supply chain expert. He was involved in many complex supply chain and logistics projects in Asia, heading the operations for many reputable multinational companies. In 2018, he won the JDA global Real Results Award with Aw.

www.ingramcontent.com/pod-product-compliance
Lightning Source LLC
Chambersburg PA
CBHW030635220526
45463CB00004B/1533